EATING DISORDERS IN THE 21ST CENTURY

ANOREXIA NERVOSA

SYMPTOMS, TREATMENT, AND NEUROBIOLOGY

EATING DISORDERS IN THE 21ST CENTURY

Additional books in this series can be found on Nova's website under the Series tab.

Additional e-books in this series can be found on Nova's website under the e-books tab.

EATING DISORDERS IN THE 21ST CENTURY

ANOREXIA NERVOSA

SYMPTOMS, TREATMENT, AND NEUROBIOLOGY

NICOLE C. BARBARICH-MARSTELLER
EDITOR

Nova Science Publishers, Inc.
New York

For permission to use material from this book please contact us:
Telephone 631-231-7269; Fax 631-231-8175
Web Site: http://www.novapublishers.com

Library of Congress Cataloging-in-Publication Data

ISBN: 978-1-62081-291-4
Library of Congress Control Number: 2012933656

Published by Nova Science Publishers, Inc. † New York

CONTENTS

PREFACE

Anorexia Nervosa is an enigmatic and, too commonly, an extremely challenging disorder. Its core clinical features have been recognized for centuries, and the label anorexia nervosa was coined in the 19th century. Over the many ensuing years, the disorder has been examined from a wide variety of perspectives, ranging from psychoanalytic to genetic. While potential risk factors have been identified, features clarified and complications appreciated, a full understanding and universally effective methods of treatment remain elusive. The current volume does not attempt to review the long history of research on anorexia nervosa. Rather, leaders in the field describe fresh approaches and new directions. This volume is a very forward-looking examination of novel ideas and new approaches to the understanding of an old, extremely persistent and enigmatic mental disorder. The approaches described will hopefully form a foundation for significant advances in the years ahead.

Chapter 1 - The longitudinal course of anorexia nervosa (AN) is marked by symptom fluctuation and resultant "crossover" both within AN (i.e., between AN subtypes) and between eating disorder diagnoses (e.g., from AN to bulimia nervosa [BN]). Longitudinal research suggests that crossover typically reflects the transition from a primarily restrictive to a bingeing and/or purging presentation. Specifically, the majority of those with restricting type AN develop binge/purge type AN during the course of their illness, and up to 50% of those initially diagnosed with AN develop bulimic symptoms over time. Crossover is frequent, recurrent, and can occur bi-directionally. The phenomenon of crossover challenges the validity of the current classification system of eating disorders, calling into question the accuracy of the initial diagnosis or subtype assignment, and suggesting that the boundaries between eating disorder diagnoses and subtypes may need to be redrawn. From a clinical perspective, psychoeducation on the likelihood of diagnostic crossover may be therapeutic for patients who idealize the restrictive state, and understanding the impact of crossover on clinical communication, treatment selection, and recovery definition is critical. With regard to research, crossover patterns inform nosological conceptualizations, and in turn etiologic inquiry, as well as definitions of longitudinal outcome.

Chapter 2 - To examine the latent structure of anorexia nervosa, restricting type, the authors applied three taxometric procedures (MAMBAC, MAXEIG, and LMODE) to a sample of n = 196 anorexic women and n = 1092 female undergraduate students. Indicators for anorexia nervosa were body mass index and items taken from the Eating Attitudes Test-26. In analyses usinga mixed sample, the results were consistently suggestive of a latent taxon for anorexia nervosa. However, in the undergraduate sample, results were less conclusive and more consistent with a dimensional model suggesting that the findings from the mixed sample may have been artifactual. The findings have implications for etiological models of eating disorders, for assessment of anorexia nervosa and for future taxometric research on anorexia nervosa or other eating disorders.

Chapter 3 - Excessive physical activity is often observed in patients with Anorexia Nervosa (AN) and may contribute to significant clinical difficulties. Physical activity may assume a range of forms including pacing, fidgeting and exercise behavior. This chapter will review the manifestations and clinical correlates of excessive physical activity in people with AN, as well as possible treatment implications. The animal model of "Activity Based Anorexia" will be presented in light of its relevance to the clinical phenomenon of excessive physical activity in AN.

Chapter 4 - Anorexia nervosa (AN) is a serious psychiatric disorder that affects approximately .05% of the population. AN has the highest mortality rate of any psychiatric disorder, and is associated with adverse physical and psychosocial health outcomes. Despite its public health significance, there is a dearth of efficacy data on treatments for AN. Various interventions have been developed, but few have generated successful outcomes in randomized controlled trials. The purpose of this chapter is to systematically review existing evidence-based psychosocial treatments for AN in adolescents and adults. The current literature suggests that family-based treatment is the most efficacious intervention for adolescent AN, as it is associated with significant increases in body weight and psychological functioning across trials. To date, there is no clear treatment of choice for adult AN; thus, identifying efficacious treatments for adults with AN should be a priority. For adolescents, future research should examine alternative interventions for those who fail to respond to family-based treatment.

Chapter 5 - Despite the high rates of comorbidity with depression and anxiety disorders, as well as the significant neurotransmitter alterations present during starvation, pharmacological treatments targeting the serotonin and dopamine system have had surprisingly little efficacy in the treatment of anorexia nervosa. As this chapter reviews, there is no clear evidence to support the use of typical antipsychotics or antidepressants in the treatment of anorexia nervosa. While atypical antipsychotics provide the most promising line of pharmacological treatment when used as an adjunct to other treatments, these drugs are only effective for some individuals with anorexia nervosa. Additional research is clearly needed to identify the biological systems that perpetuate the unrelenting self-starvation in individuals with anorexia nervosa, in order to develop targeted pharmacological treatments aimed at modulating the maladaptive behaviors characteristic of this deadly disease.

Chapter 6 - Anorexia nervosa (AN) is a severe psychiatric disorder that is associated with abnormalities of brain structure and function. There are a variety of brain imaging techniques that have been used to study AN giving us new insights into altered brain function in this disorder that could be related to pathologic behavior. For instance, radioligand imaging could identify alterations in brain neurotransmitter function, and studies using tasks that apply food or body image related stimuli could elicit altered response in fear or reward circuitry. In this chapter the authors review the available literature on the various findings and how such alterations may be related to the pathophysiology of the disorder.

Chapter 7 - A common denominator for all anorexia nervosa individuals is rejection of food despite the fact that the organism is in critical need of replenishing energy. Interestingly, not only do hunger mechanisms prove insufficient to stimulate consumption, but also rewarding properties of tastants do not serve as an adequate incentive to motivate eating. In addition, negative associations with consequences of consummatory activity are common in this disease. Intriguingly, food avoidance in anorexia nervosa mirrors characteristic features of taste aversion in animal models: negative associations with food intake cause self-starvation despite hunger and tastant's palatability. Recent studies have shown that taste aversion in rodents is associated with profound changes in central expression of genes related to food intake, including genes mediating feeding for energy and those involved in reward. It is particularly striking that administration of ligands that modify reward affects the magnitude of an aversive response, being able to reinforce or, importantly, to alleviate food avoidance. The current chapter offers a perspective on using our knowledge of taste aversion in animal models to better understand the biology of anorexia nervosa and on possible directions in conceptualizing pharmacologic interventions.

Chapter 8 - Anorexia nervosa, with a mortality rate of 5% per decade of illness, ranks among the most lethal of psychiatric disorders.The potential for the development of more effective treatments for this illness would be greatly enhanced if the mechanisms maintaining the abnormal behaviors characteristic of anorexia nervosa were better understood.Preclinical models of human illnesses can provide a unique opportunity to probe physiological mechanisms and to test pharmacotherapies.While it is not possible to fully model the complexity of any psychiatric disorder, an animal model of anorexia nervosa could significantly advance our understanding and treatment of this challenging disorder.This chapter discusses the utility of using a translational model of anorexia nervosa to understand the biology of self-starvation and starvation-induced hyperactivity.

In: Anorexia Nervosa
Editor: N. C. Barbarich-Marsteller
ISBN: 978-1-62081-291-4

Chapter 1

DIAGNOSTIC CROSSOVER

***Caitlin M. Nevins*[a], *Kamryn T. Eddy*[*b,c,d] and *Jennifer J. Thomas*[a,b,d]**

[a]Klarman Eating Disorders Center, McLean Hospital, Belmont, MA, US
[b]Department of Psychiatry, Harvard Medical School, Boston, MA, US
[c]Harris Center for Education and Advocacy in Eating Disorders, Massachusetts General Hospital, Boston, MA, US
[d]Eating Disorders Clinical and Research Program, Massachusetts General Hospital, Boston, MA, US

ABSTRACT

The longitudinal course of anorexia nervosa (AN) is marked by symptom fluctuation and resultant "crossover" both within AN (i.e., between AN subtypes) and between eating disorder diagnoses (e.g., from AN to bulimia nervosa [BN]). Longitudinal research suggests that crossover typically reflects the transition from a primarily restrictive to a bingeing and/or purging presentation. Specifically, the majority of those with restricting type AN develop binge/purge type AN during the course of their illness, and up to 50% of those initially diagnosed with AN develop bulimic symptoms over time. Crossover is frequent, recurrent, and can occur bi-directionally. The phenomenon of crossover challenges the validity of the current classification system of eating disorders, calling

* Massachusetts General Hospital, 2 Longfellow Place, Suite 200, Boston, MA 02114, (617) 724-1744, keddy@partners.org

into question the accuracy of the initial diagnosis or subtype assignment, and suggesting that the boundaries between eating disorder diagnoses and subtypes may need to be redrawn. From a clinical perspective, psychoeducation on the likelihood of diagnostic crossover may be therapeutic for patients who idealize the restrictive state, and understanding the impact of crossover on clinical communication, treatment selection, and recovery definition is critical. With regard to research, crossover patterns inform nosological conceptualizations, and in turn etiologic inquiry, as well as definitions of longitudinal outcome.

Introduction

The DSM-IV currently recognizes three distinct eating disorder (ED) diagnoses: anorexia nervosa (AN), bulimia nervosa (BN) and eating disorder not otherwise specified (EDNOS). AN is characterized by low body weight (e.g., less than 85% of that expected for age and height), intense fear of weight gain, body image disturbance, and amenorrhea. Restricting type AN (AN-R) criteria specify that "weight loss is accomplished primarily through dieting, fasting or excessive exercise" and require that "individuals have not regularly engaged in binge eating or purging" [1]. Binge/purge type AN (AN-BP) is "used when the individual has regularly engaged in binge eating or purging" [1] though DSM-IV notes that "sufficient information is not available to justify the specification of a minimum frequency" for these behaviors [1]. In contrast, BN is characterized by recurrent binge eating (i.e., consuming large amounts of food while feeling out of control) and purging (e.g., self-induced vomiting, abuse of laxatives or diuretics, fasting, or compensatory exercise) at normal- or over-weight, and basing self-worth disproportionately on shape and weight [1]. EDNOS is a broader diagnostic category that includes all other clinically significant ED presentations that do not meet full criteria for either AN nor BN.

Phenomenon of Diagnostic Crossover

According to DSM-IV, only one ED diagnosis can be conferred at any given time, which challenges clinicians and researchers to apply the criteria to best match a patient's *current* symptom presentation. Given the overlapping clinical profiles across ED diagnoses, a trump system specifies that a patient with AN who would also meet criteria for BN should be given a single diagnosis of AN-BP for parsimony. Yet for those with EDs, the longitudinal course of illness is marked by symptom fluctuation (e.g., periods of restricting followed by periods of binge eating and/or purging; waxing and waning of symptom severity), and DSM-IV does not provide guidance on the bounds of these disorders to recognize when a patient no longer has a given diagnosis either because she has recovered or developed a *different ED type*. In the literature, diagnostic crossover is a term that has been used to define movement within ED subtypes (e.g., AN-R and AN-BP) or between ED diagnoses (e.g., AN and BN).

While an individual can be assigned only one initial ED diagnosis (i.e., AN, BN or EDNOS), even minor fluctuations in symptom presentation may lead to diagnostic crossover when the criteria are strictly applied. For example, an individual who maintains a low weight by restricting food intake for many years and eventually initiates regular self-induced vomiting would be re-classified from AN-R to AN-BP. Similarly, a low-weight individual who regularly binges and purges may cross over from AN-BP to BN with a modicum of weight gain. Continued symptom fluctuation across the course of the illness may then lead to bidirectional and recurrent re-classification across ED diagnoses [2].

Operationalizing Diagnostic Crossover

A small body of nosological studies has examined the frequency and predictors of diagnostic crossover [2-13] These efforts highlight some of the challenges in studying crossover including inconsistent definitions of key diagnostic criteria. Since DSM-IV defines AN subtypes in general terms [14], each study must determine its own guidelines. For example, one study operationalized the onset of "regular" binge-purge behavior — and, therefore, crossover from AN-R to AN-BP — as at least once weekly for eight consecutive weeks [5]. However, other studies have used alternative definitions, including bingeing and/or purging at least once every two weeks for three months [9]. With respect to crossover from AN to BN, myriad potential methods for calculating expected body weight (e.g., Metropolitan Life Insurance tables; body mass index [BMI] percentiles) render the operationalization of low versus normal body weight similarly challenging [15].

Importance of Diagnostic Crossover

It is important to further examine crossover among ED diagnoses in order to better understand illness presentation in general. Diagnoses are designed to inform clinicians and researchers about the course of illness. If symptoms change over time, it may become difficult for clinicians to effectively communicate with one another. Furthermore, it may be difficult to present to the patient what to expect in terms of risks, course of illness, and effective treatments methods. Fluidity between AN and BN is important not only to the understanding of symptom presentation over time, but also to the proposed treatment of EDs. Treatment methodologies are typically developed to address a specific diagnostic category, and, as a result, show differential effectiveness across ED diagnoses. For example, Cognitive Behavioral Therapy (CBT) is a highly effective treatment for BN [16-18], yet there is less evidence for its effectiveness in the treatment of AN [19,20]. Given the high crossover frequency between AN and BN, treatment methods may be more effective if they account for the repeated finding that ED diagnoses change over time.

A better understanding of crossover will also enhance research methodology. The majority of ED research studies are cross-sectional. If many individuals have a prior history of, or will go on to develop, a different ED diagnosis, the inferences drawn about diagnostic groups made from study diagnosis alone may lack internal validity. Furthermore, longitudinal studies may provide limited information about illness course if they do not account for the crossover that appears to occur in the first few years of illness onset [7, 12]. Thus, continued research on diagnostic crossover will allow for a better understanding of the plasticity of AN and BN as well as changes in illness presentation over time.

Frequency of Diagnostic Crossover

Extant research has raised questions about the longitudinal stability of ED phenotypes as defined in DSM-IV. Table 1 summarizes the results of eleven studies since the 1994 publication of DSM-IV that have either retrospectively or prospectively evaluated diagnostic crossover among patients with an initial (or study entry) diagnosis of AN. As depicted in Table 1, crossover has been observed from AN to every other DSM-IV ED category.

Table 1. Retrospective and prospective studies studies reporting diagnostic crossover among patients with a study entry diagnosis of Anorexia Nervosa

Author	Length of Follow-up (Years)	Diagnostic Assessment	*N* at Follow-up	Crossover Rate (%)[a]
		Retrospective Studies		
Tozzi et al., 2005	N/A	SIAB for DSM-IV and ICD-10	AN-R = 88	AN → BN (36%)
Anderluh et al., 2008	N/A	EATATE Lifetime Diagnostic Review	AN-R = 55 AN-BP/P = 24	AN-R → AN-BP (2%) AN-P → BN-P (4%) AN-BP → BN-P (4%)
Monteleone et al., 2011	N/A	SCID	AN-R = 70 AN-BP = 45	AN-R → BN (34%) AN-BP → BN (51%)
		Prospective Studies		
Ecket et al., 1995	10	Anorectic Outcome Scale	AN = 71	AN → BN (24%) AN → EDNOS (38%)
Strober et al., 1997	10 to 15	LIFE	AN = 95	AN → BN (10%)
Milos et al., 2005	2.5	SCID	AN = 55	AN → BN (9%) AN → EDNOS (20%)
Fichter et al., 2006[b]	12	SIAB-EX	AN = 91	AN → BN (9%) AN → EDNOS (18%)
Eddy et al., 2008[b,c]	7	LIFE EAT-II	AN-R = 40 AN-BP = 48	AN-R → AN-BP (10%) AN-R → BN (2%) AN-BP → AN-R (13%) AN-BP → BN (13%)
van Son et al., 2010[c]	4.8	ED symptoms as reported by each patient's primary care physician	AN-R = 28 AN-BP = 46	AN-BP → BN (6%) AN-BP → EDNOS (6%)
Rigaud et al., 2011	13	Self-report questionnaire based on EDE-Q and EDI	AN-R = 411 AN-BP = 73	AN-R → AN-BP or BN (31%) AN-BP → BN (3%)
Castelinni et al., 2011	6	SCID	AN = 165	AN → BN (27%) AN → AN or EDNOS (21%)

a All rates of crossover in prospective studies reported in this table represent crossover from initial study diagnosis to a new diagnosis at a single follow-up point for parsimony. Limitations of summarizing crossover by a single follow-up point are reviewed in the text.

b Fichter et al., 2007 not included because reports on same sample as Fichter et al., 2006; Eddy et al., 2002 and Eddy et al., 2010 not included because both report on same sample as Eddy et al., 2008.

Note. LIFE = Longitudinal Interval Follow-up Evaluation; LIFE EAT-II = LIFE, Eating Disorders Version; SIAB = Structured Inventory for Anorexic and Bulimic Syndromes; EDE-Q = Eating Disorder Examination-Questionnaire; EDI = Eating Disorder Inventory; SCID-IV = Structured Clinical Interview for DSM-IV

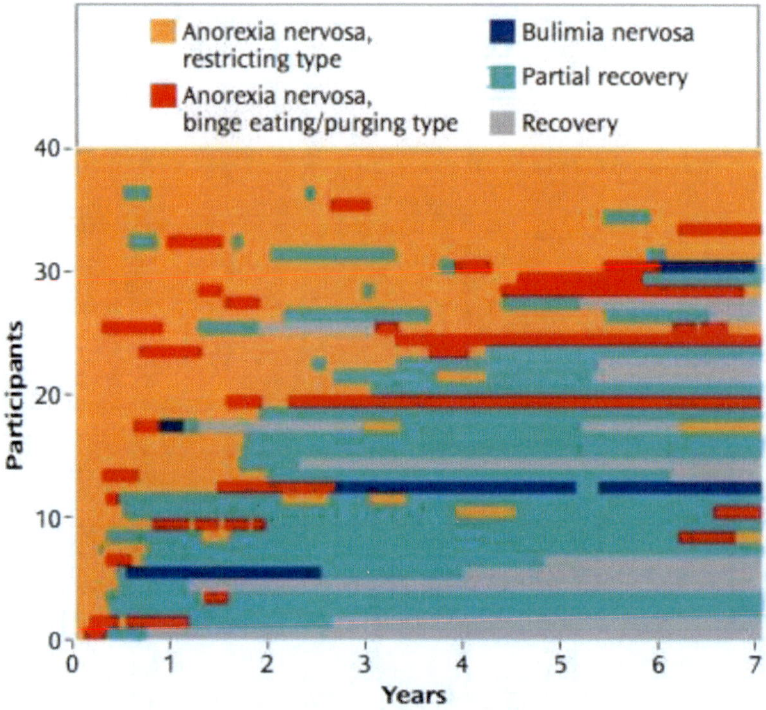

[a] Each row in the figure represents one participant.

Note: Figure is reprinted with permission from [American Psychiatric Association (Journals) via Copyright Clearance Center].

Figure 1. Longitudinal Course and Crossover for Participants With an Intake Diagnosis of Anorexia Nervosa, Restricting Type ($N = 40$) from Eddy et al. (2008).

The most frequent trend to be both studied and observed is migration from AN-R to AN-BP [2, 5, 8, 12]. In a seven-year follow-up study of diagnostic crossover in AN and BN, nearly half (49%) those participants with a study entry diagnosis of AN experienced crossover between the two AN subtypes at some point during follow-up [2]. In another study, 31% of participants with an initial diagnosis of AN-R crossed over, at varying points in time, to either AN-BP or BN over the course of 13 years [12]. Crossover is most common within the first three [12] to five [7] years of ED onset, prompting some investigators to speculate that AN-R is a preliminary phase of AN-BP and even BN [5].

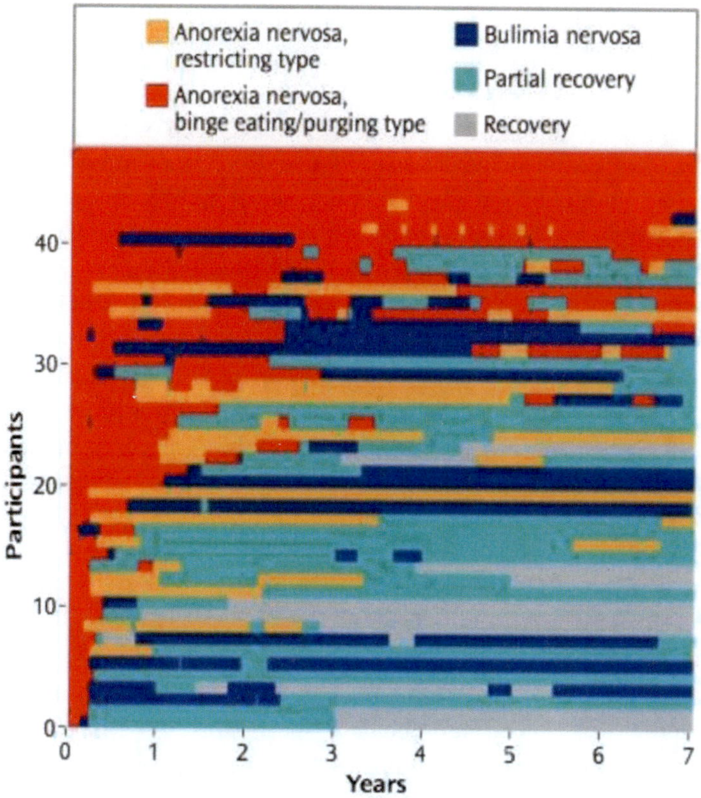

[a] Each row in the figure represents one participant.

Note: Figure is reprinted with permission from [American Psychiatric Association (Journals) via Copyright Clearance Center].

Figure 2. Longitudinal Course and Crossover for Participants With an Intake Diagnosis of Anorexia Nervosa, Binge/Purge Type (*N* = 48) from Eddy et al. (2008).

Indeed, crossover from AN to BN is also commonly observed [2, 4, 7, 8, 10, 12, 21]. While an initial diagnosis of AN-R has demonstrated some crossover to BN [2, 12], available data suggest that BN is more likely to develop from AN-BP [9, 11]. For example, in a seven-year follow up study, 54% of participants with AN-BP at study entry crossed over to BN, compared to just 10% of those with AN-R; further, those with AN-R who did cross over to BN, did so after first crossing over to AN-BP [2]. Unlike the well-documented crossover from AN to BN, there is little evidence of diagnostic crossover from AN to binge eating disorder (BED; a subtype of EDNOS that features recurrent binge eating in the absence of purging). In three separate reports with follow-up intervals ranging from five to nine years, crossover from AN to BED ranged from 0% [13, 22] to 2% [10].

Crossover can also be bidirectional. As exemplified in Figures 1-2, 73% of participants with an initial diagnosis of AN crossed over into a different AN subtype (49%) or developed frank BN over 7 years of follow-up (34%) over seven years of follow-up [2]. However, nearly half of the participants who crossed over to BN ultimately ended up returning back to an AN diagnosis [2]. Further, the same investigators reported that BN participants with a history of AN were more likely to cross over to AN compared with BN patients who did not have a history of AN [23]. These findings suggest that in spite of symptom fluctuation – and in particular weight gain or loss – patients with a history of AN may be vulnerable to returning to a low weight over time. These findings incite the suggestion that lifetime AN history be recognized in those patients who present for the treatment of BN, perhaps by a subtyping wherein those with BN are typed as with or without a history of AN [23].

Limitations of Crossover Data

Available data on ED crossover are limited by variations in research methodology and reporting schemes. Specifically, different methodologies appear to promote different conclusions about crossover frequency. For example, a study that evaluated ED symptoms documented by individual primary care physicians detected no crossover between AN and BN at final follow-up [10]. In contrast, a study that used a more valid and reliable assessment tool — the Structured Clinical Interview for DSM-IV (SCID-IV; [24]) — found that 27% of participants crossed over from AN to BN at final follow-up over a similar period of time [13]. Moreover, studies utilizing frequent follow-ups (e.g., annual or semi-annual), which increase sensitivity, typically report higher rates of crossover [2, 4, 5, 22] than those that allow for longer gaps between assessments. This interpretation of the data is supported by one study [12], where 17% of AN-Rs developed AN-BP or BN during intermediate assessments, but the vast majority were recovered by the final 13-year follow-up. However, in some cases, more rigorous methodologies identify lower rates of crossover. Retrospective studies (e.g., [7, 9, 11]), which have the advantage of considering crossover at any point in the lifetime, typically report higher rates of crossover than prospective studies; yet retrospective designs may be limited by participant recall bias and less thorough clinical assessment of past symptoms.

Crossover rates may stabilize if future studies employ the most rigorous possible methodological features, including prospective designs; valid and reliable assessments that are specifically designed to capture temporal variation; multiple intermediate time points; and long follow-up periods. For example, assessment tools such as the Structured Interview for Anorexic and Bulimic Symptoms (SIAB-EX; [25]) or the Longitudinal Interval Follow-up Evaluation of Eating Disorders (LIFE EAT-II; [26]), which systematically probe for both current and past symptoms, will likely yield more valid data than physician report or questionnaires. Prospective studies utilizing such interviews at multiple time points over several decades will optimize sensitivity to validly capture the true longitudinal course of AN.

Prediction of Diagnostic Crossover

The typical direction of diagnostic migration (i.e., movement from restrictive to bulimic presentations over time) may have both physiological and psychological underpinnings. Physiological factors are clearly demonstrated in the 1944 Minnesota starvation experiment, in which 36 male participants were taken through three phases: a control period to determine baseline behavior, a starvation period with significant calorie reduction, and finally a recovery and re-feeding phase [27]. During both the starvation and re-feeding periods, participants' presentations were similar to the constellation of attitudes and behaviors associated with disordered eating. Specifically, the men became overly preoccupied with food as their interest in other activities declined. They reported increased hunger and also experienced "a complete breakdown in control," leading them to binge on large quantities of food, sometimes followed by vomiting and often followed by self-deprecation (p. 156, [27]). Binge-like behaviors following restrictive periods have also been observed in animal models of disordered eating, in which caloric restriction coupled with environmental stress has led to a "powerful increase in food intake" in female rates (p. 52, [28]).

Along with the physiological effects, there is also psychological support for the unsustainable nature of restrictive eating behaviors. Available data support the theory that self-control has a limited supply, similar to that of physical strength: Heavy exertion of self-control typically results in a period of self-regulatory depletion, or a decreased ability to exert self-control on subsequent tasks [29]. The notion of self-control as a limited resource has been empirically tested in relation to eating behavior [30]. Chronic dieters were placed in either a low-temptation setting or a high-temptation setting. In the high-temptation setting, participants were told they could eat as many snacks as they wanted, requiring them to exert self-control so as not derail their diets. This effort to refrain from the snacks resulted in decreased self-control when participants were later given the opportunity to eat as much ice cream as they wanted (in one study) and decreased persistence on an unsolvable math problem (in a second study) [30]. These results are consistent with the notion that long-term starvation may be psychologically unsustainable, ultimately leading to self-regulatory depletion (e.g., binge eating), as observed in the crossover from AN-R to AN-BP and/or BN.

In light of these physiological and psychological findings, it is notable that a subset of AN-R patients never cross over into AN-BP or BN. A previous longitudinal study of AN [11] identified higher lifetime BMI, and lower self-directedness (the lack of internal organization and the lack of the ability to pursue lasting and meaningful goals; [31]) as harbingers of crossover from restrictive to binge/purge presentations. It is important to further explore the similarities in diagnoses that may lead to crossover, as well as the differences between patients with distinctive longitudinal trajectories. Clinicians, researchers, and patients will benefit from a better understanding of how and why symptom presentation may change over the course of the illness.

CLINICAL IMPLICATIONS

The high rates of diagnostic crossover observed in longitudinal studies of AN have important therapeutic implications for diagnostic assessment, clinical communication, motivational enhancement, treatment selection, and outcome evaluation.

Diagnostic Assessment

Because crossover is so prevalent, evaluating an ED patient's symptoms at treatment presentation can be likened to reading a single chapter from a suspense novel: Major plot threads may be overlooked. Thus the importance of assessing lifetime symptoms in the initial clinical assessment cannot be overemphasized. Given that a prior history of AN among patients with BN predicts its re-emergence [23], querying minimum and maximum weights at current height may be particularly informative. Similarly, because AN-BP may be associated with increased psychiatric comorbidity [32] and additional medical risk [33], it is important to query for lifetime bingeing and purging in patients with current AN-R. To that end, clinicians should appreciate the time limitations embedded in the field's most valid and reliable assessment tools. Even the widely used Eating Disorder Examination interview [34] assesses symptoms over the past six months only. Therefore, we recommend that clinicians always append open-ended items that probe for lifetime symptoms beyond those queried in traditional diagnostic timeframes. Lastly, in light of the secrecy and shame surrounding bulimic symptoms [35], physicians may wish to run laboratory tests with the potential to detect covert purging (e.g., serum amylase, bicarbonate, potassium; [33]), even among patients who present with apparent AN-R.

Clinical Communication

Optimally, psychiatric diagnoses should serve as clinical shorthand to facilitate rapid communication of mutual expectations about symptom presentation, likely prognosis, and optimal treatment [36]. Unfortunately, ED diagnoses that lack temporal stability may confuse rather than clarify these issues. Thus clinicians should take care to factor in diagnostic history when referring patients and planning treatment. For example, a clinician receiving a referral of an EDNOS patient might wish to plan a more intensive treatment regimen if the patient has a known history of AN; a recent meta-analysis identified a higher mortality rate in AN compared to either BN or EDNOS [37].

Motivational Enhancement

Many ED patients are ambivalent about recovery [38]. Reluctance to relinquish restrictive behaviors in particular is predictive of poor treatment outcome [39]. Gentle psychoeducation about the likelihood and direction of diagnostic crossover can be used therapeutically to enhance motivation for change among patients with both AN-R and AN-BP.

Specifically, many AN-R patients worry that if they even slightly increase their caloric intake to facilitate weight restoration, they will completely lose control over their eating. According to Knapp (2003) in her memoir of AN, "My great terror during the early years of therapy [was] …that if I escaped the anorexic prison and truly surrendered all that hard-won control over appetite… I'd be so consumed with need and desire that I'd never stop eating" (p. 190, [40]). Such patients should be reminded that they are actually at highest risk for binge eating while they remain underweight. To that end, Fairburn (2008, [34]) recommends that even AN-R patients be asked to read the self-help manual *Overcoming Binge Eating* [41], which underscores the likelihood that continued dietary restriction will lead to bingeing, or even frank BN, over time. Taking a slightly more conservative tack, Waller et al. (2007, [42]) suggests challenging AN-R patients' fear of losing control by asking Socratic questions such as, "Before you developed your eating disorder, when you were still eating regularly, did you feel out of control in the way that you do right now?" (p. 151).

In contrast, AN-BP and BN patients often idealize the initial AN-R "honeymoon" phase during which they were temporarily able to maintain strict control over their eating. These patients identify bulimia as their primary problem, and hope that can ultimately return to AN-R once they have successfully stopped bingeing and purging. Hornbacher (1998, [43]) highlights the appeal of restrictive symptoms in her memoir of AN and BN (i.e., "I wanted to be an anoretic… a person whose passions were ascetic rather than hedonistic," p. 107), but later recounts with shame the physiological inevitability of binge eating after periods of prolonged restriction: "at some point, the body will essentially eat of its own accord in order to save itself. …It feels very much as if you are possessed, as if you have no will of your own but are in constant battle with your body, and you are losing" (p. 267). ED patients who idealize their AN-R phase may benefit from psychoeducation about the factors that keep them locked in to AN-BP or BN. For example, Fairburn (2008, [44]) highlights the cyclic nature of ED symptoms in his transdiagnostic cognitive-behavioral model: Patients who redouble their efforts at dieting in order to compensate for binge episodes may be unwittingly setting the stage for their very next binge.

Treatment Selection

Frequent migration across ED diagnostic categories is suggestive of shared psychopathology [45], which may provide partial support for the use of transdiagnostic treatments [41, 44]. Fairburn's "enhanced" CBT (CBT-E; [44]) recommends creating a personalized formulation that takes into account each patient's unique symptom presentation. In cases where diagnostic crossover has been present, constructing the whole CBT-E transdiagnostic formulation may be particularly valuable. When presenting this model, it can be useful to provide both a "micro" and "macro" view of ED maintenance mechanisms (i.e., just as under-eating early in the day may lead to binge eating later that evening, chronic food restriction earlier in the illness may lead to chronic binge eating later in the illness) to engage patients in the process of change.

Outcome Evaluation

Appreciation of the typical timing and direction of crossover can help clinicians evaluate the outcomes of their treatment interventions. Given that patient and clinician goals may differ to some extent, it is important that clinicians do not mistake crossover (a poor outcome) for remission (an ideal outcome). Indeed, Keski-Rahkonen and Tozzi [46] refer to the maintenance of low weight after the cessation of binge/purge behaviors (i.e., crossover from AN-BP to AN-R) as "pseudo-recovery." Although the patient may be satisfied with this outcome, the therapist must insist that the maintenance of a low weight leaves the patient highly vulnerable to relapse.

Research Implications

The frequent, bidirectional, and recurrent nature of ED crossover has important implications for nosologic, etiologic, and outcomes research.

Nosologic Conceptualization

The most obvious implication of high rates of diagnostic crossover is to challenge the existing classification system. DSM-IV diagnoses are assigned on the basis of current presentation to facilitate communication about and study of specific clinical presentations, and to convey information with regard to prognosis and course of illness. The AN subtyping system was initially established to recognize observed cross-sectional differences between individuals who regularly engage in binge/purge behaviors and those who do not, including impulsivity, psychiatric comorbidity, and degree of medical risk where low weight is compounded by purging [1, 32]. However, subsequent studies found that those with AN-R were frequently younger with a shorter duration of illness relative to those with AN-BP, suggesting that AN-R may be an earlier phase in the course of AN-BP (e.g., [5]). Furthermore, longitudinal research indicating that a subset of those with AN-R eventually develop AN-BP, and that many of those with AN-BP experience periods of abstinence from binge/purge behavior, provided further support for the phase model. These findings suggest that the cross-sectional AN subtyping system, which will continue in DSM-5 [47], is not longitudinally stable and may be limited in its ability to convey information about expected course and outcome.

Yet taken as a whole, the crossover literature also suggests that there may be meaningful heterogeneity within the AN diagnosis: A subset of those with AN-R will not develop binge/purge symptoms regardless of follow-up duration, and AN-R patients are less likely than AN-BP patients to develop BN over time. Further, those with BN who have a history of AN are more likely than those with no AN history to relapse to AN and, in particular, to relapse to AN-BP [23].

A research strategy that has widely been applied in the field of EDs to investigate nosology in the last decade is the use of statistical approaches, such as latent class or latent profile analyses (LCA/LPA), to empirically derive alternative classification schemes that can be directly tested against DSM-IV (see [48] for review). To date, these studies have used clinical indicators of current or lifetime ED psychopathology to identify latent groups. The crossover literature would support the inclusion of both current *and* lifetime symptoms as indicators — particularly lowest lifetime weight — and would also suggest the value of examining the predictive validity of any identified groups (i.e., their ability to predict longitudinal course and outcome) in comparison to existing DSM categories. Further, approaches such as latent transition analysis (LTA) and latent growth mixture modeling (LGMM) when applied to comprehensive longitudinal datasets, can be used to identify latent groups on the basis of longitudinal symptom patterns. These longitudinal statistical techniques have been applied in the study of other psychiatric disorders but to date few studies have used these techniques in EDs [49-51] and none of these were utilized for the purposes of diagnostic classification. These approaches could be useful in clarifying boundaries between latent groups that account for longitudinal symptom course.

However, if there are important subgroups within the diagnostic category of AN, reliance on clinical symptoms — which are transient — to identify them may be inadequate. A recent report from the National Institute of Mental Health (NIMH, [52]) calls for biologically-oriented research aimed at elucidating the neural pathophysiology of EDs [53], which may prove useful in clarifying latent groups. Strategy 1.4 of the NIMH Strategic Plan impels, "the development, for research purposes, of new ways of classifying psychopathology based on dimensions of observable behavior and neurobiological measures" [52]. The framework for this approach, RDoC (Research Domain Criteria), is that the identification of neurobiological underpinnings of psychiatric disorders may help to inform alternative classification schemes that have incremental validity over the current system.

One application of this strategy that could build on the crossover research would examine neuropsychological or neurobiological patterns in individuals with EDs transdiagnostically (e.g., across the AN subtypes, and across all EDs) wherein it may be possible to identify subgroups of individuals with EDs not easily identifiable by current clinical profile. It is possible that a range of cognitive processes — including reward sensitivity, affect regulation, and inhibitory control, for example — all of which have been studied in EDs (see [54] for review), may help to clarify the heterogeneity within EDs, and specifically within AN. For example, in AN, phenotype characteristics including perfectionism, obsessionality, cognitive and behavioral inflexibility, risk aversion, and asceticism, may reflect an underlying dysregulation in inhibitory control processes. While individuals with AN-R are exquisitely skilled at resisting impulses to eat, they can conversely be considered unskilled at inhibiting obsessional weight/shape cognitions or compulsions to count calories or over-exercise. Further, individuals with AN-R have great difficulty breaking out of their restrictive eating patterns in order to initiate healthy alternative behaviors and often have limited motivation for treatment. Conversely, many will experience lapses in restraint with the onset of binge eating or purging. One possible avenue of exploration is the study of such cognitive processes and associated neural patterns that may differentiate subtypes wherein AN-R may be associated with relatively more cognitive and behavioral compulsivity, while those who are prone to current or future AN-BP would demonstrate more impulsivity.

Etiology

Multidimensional risk factor models of EDs consider biological, psychological, and social variables. While all of these factors are thought to play a role in the development of AN, its etiology remains unknown and etiological research efforts may be hindered in part by an imperfect classification system. The shared clinical features across the EDs, and longitudinal diagnostic crossover findings, support the notion of examining global factors that increase risk for all EDs. Further, the crossover literature argues for inquiry into specific factors that increase risk for the development of certain symptom profiles and disorders at different times. For example, among the population of individuals with AN-R, a subset will remain chronic restrictors while another will develop binge/purge behaviors. Inquiry into the risk factors associated both with the development and timing of onset of binge/purge behaviors could be informative, and to date very few predictors of crossover have been identified.

Research aimed at examining biological underpinnings of EDs for nosologic purposes can also be used in guiding etiologic studies. While it has proven to be difficult to identify individual genes associated with the ED phenotypes or individual clinical symptoms (e.g., [55]), RDoC-informed research strategies may help to identify neuropsychological or neurobiological underpinnings that could represent endophenotypes of these illnesses. Endophenotypes are considered to be intermediate between the observable phenotype and the genotype; thus, if there are distinctive patterns or latent groups that emerge through such research, genetic inquiry can be guided by these findings.

Longitudinal Outcome

How to define longitudinal outcomes — partial and full recovery, crossover to a new diagnosis — is a challenge in the ED field and there are no universally accepted definitions [56, 57]. In addition to its clinical implications, the data documenting longitudinal symptom fluctuation can also inform the study of outcomes. Should those with AN-R who develop binge/purge symptoms be re-defined as having AN-BP, and if they subsequently return to primarily restricting behavior should their subtype revert to AN-R? Perhaps more importantly, should those with AN-BP who begin to restore weight such that they no longer meet the AN weight criterion be re-classified as BN? If so, should their history of AN be noted, perhaps with a diagnostic specifier? Further, DSM-IV does not provide guidelines on how to classify individuals previously diagnosed with AN or BN who remain symptomatic but no longer meet full criteria for either of these disorders. Should these individuals retain the initial diagnosis of AN or BN — and perhaps be described as in partial recovery — or should they be assigned a separate diagnosis of EDNOS?

The crossover literature suggests that symptomatic change — and in some cases improvement — is part of the natural course of AN or BN and thus seems to be better captured as part of the same illness, rather than constituting a new diagnosis [22]. Studies that include comprehensive longitudinal assessment both of symptoms and of clinically meaningful validators that could help to clarify boundaries between the ED diagnoses are needed. Future research using sensitive measures of clinical distress or impairment may also help to clarify boundaries between threshold ED, partial recovery, and full recovery [22, 56].

Conclusion

Diagnostic crossover in AN is common. It typically features migration from restrictive to binge/purge presentations, and most often occurs within the first three to five years of illness onset. Exact rates of crossover are inconclusive due to the methodological heterogeneity of extant literature. We therefore recommend that future studies use prospective designs; reliable and valid diagnostic interviews; annual or semi-annual assessments; and multi-decade follow-up periods. Such research is critical given the clinical implications of crossover for diagnostic assessment, clinical communication, motivational enhancement, treatment selection, and outcome evaluation.

Longitudinal studies of AN and BN highlight three distinctive clinical presentations: (1) a small group with AN-R who will never develop binge/purge symptoms, (2) a larger group with "mixed" presentations over time (i.e., fluctuating between AN-R, AN-BP, and BN), and (3) a third group with BN who have never experienced AN. Because these groups are not adequately captured in our present-focused DSM-IV or DSM-5 taxonomy, RDoC-informed research strategies may help us identify the neuropsychological or neurobiological endophenotypes that underlie these discrete longitudinal trajectories. Such findings have the potential to pave the way for improved psychological and pharmacologic treatment strategies that will reduce the burden of suffering from this high-morality psychiatric illness.

References

[1] American Psychiatric Association (2000). *Diagnostic and statistical manual of mental disorders* (4th ed., Text Revision). Washington, DC.

[2] Eddy, K. T., Dorer, D. J., Franko, D. L., Tahilani, K., Thompson-Brenner, H., & Herzog, D. B. (2008). Diagnostic crossover in anorexia nervosa and bulimia nervosa: Implications for DSM-V. *American Journal of Psychiatry, 165*(2), 245-250.

[3] Eckert, E. D., Halmi, K. A., Marchi, P., Grove, W., & Crosby, R. (1995). Ten-year follow-up of anorexia nervosa: Clinical course and outcome. *Psychological Medicine, 25*(1), 143-156.

[4] Strober, M., Freeman, R., & Morrell, W. (1997). The long-term course of severe anorexia nervosa in adolescents: Survival analysis of recovery, relapse, and outcome predictors over 10-15 years in a prospective study. *International Journal of Eating Disorders, 22*(4), 339-360

[5] Eddy, K. T., Keel, P. K., Dorer, D. J., Delinsky, S. S., Franko, D. L., & Herzog, D. B. (2002). Longitudinal comparison of anorexia nervosa subtypes. *International Journal of Eating Disorders, 31*(2), 191-201.

[6] Milos, G., Spindler, A., Schnyder, U., & Fairburn, C. G. (2005). Instability of eating disorder diagnoses: Prospective study. *British Journal of Psychiatry: The Journal of Mental Science, 187*, 573-578.

[7] Tozzi, F., Thornton, L. M., Klump, K. L., Fichter, M. M., Halmi, K. A., Kaplan, A. S., Kaye, W. H. (2005). Symptom fluctuation in eating disorders: Correlates of diagnostic crossover. *American Journal of Psychiatry, 162*(4), 732-740.

[8] Fichter, M. M., Quadflieg, N., & Hedlund, S. (2006). Twelve-year course and outcome predictors of anorexia nervosa. *International Journal of Eating Disorders, 39*(2), 87-100.

[9] Anderluh, M., Tchanturia, K., Rabe-Hesketh, S., Collier, D., & Treasure, J. (2009). Lifetime course of eating disorders: Design and validity testing of a new strategy to define the eating disorders phenotype. *Psychological Medicine, 39*(1), 105-114.

[10] van Son, G. E., van Hoeken, D., van Furth, E. F., Donker, G. A., & Hoek, H. W. (2010). Course and outcome of eating disorders in a primary care-based cohort. *International Journal of Eating Disorders, 43*(2), 130-138.

[11] Monteleone, P., Di Genio, M., Monteleone, A. M., Di Filippo, C., & Maj, M. (2011). Investigation of factors associated to crossover from anorexia nervosa restricting type (ANR) and anorexia nervosa binge-purging type (ANBP) to bulimia nervosa and comparison of bulimia nervosa patients with or without previous ANR or ANBP. *Comprehensive Psychiatry, 52*(1), 56-62.

[12] Rigaud, D., Pennacchio, H., Bizeul, C., Reveillard, V., & Verges, B. (2011). Outcome in AN adult patients: A 13-year follow-up in 484 patients. *Diabetes & Metabolism, 37(4);* 305-311.

[13] Castellini, G., Lo Sauro, C., Mannucci, E., Ravaldi, C., Rotella, C. M., Faravelli, C., & Ricca, V. (2011). Diagnostic crossover and outcome predictors in eating disorders according to DSM-IV and DSM-V proposed criteria: A 6-year follow-up study. *Psychosomatic Medicine, 73*(3), 270-279.

[14] Peat, C., Mitchell, J. E., Hoek, H. W., & Wonderlich, S. A. (2009). Validity and utility of subtyping anorexia nervosa. *International Journal of Eating Disorders, 42*(7), 590-594.

[15] Thomas, J. J., Roberto, C. A., & Brownell, K. D. (2009). Eighty-five percent of what? Discrepancies in the weight cut-off for anorexia nervosa substantially affect the prevalence of underweight. *Psychological Medicine*, 39, 833-843.

[16] Fairburn, C. G., Norman, P. A., Welch, S. L., O'Connor, M. E., Doll, H. A., & Peveler, R. C. (1995). A prospective study of outcome in bulimia nervosa and the long-term effects of three psychological treatments. *Archives of General Psychiatry, 52*(4), 304-312

[17] Agras, W. S., Walsh, T., Fairburn, C. G., Wilson, G. T., & Kraemer, H. C. (2000). A multicenter comparison of cognitive-behavioral therapy and interpersonal psychotherapy for bulimia nervosa. *Archives of General Psychiatry, 57*(5), 459-466.

[18] Fairburn, C. G., Cooper, Z., Doll, H. A., O'Connor, M. E., Bohn, K., Hawker, D. M., et al. (2009). Transdiagnostic cognitive-behavioral therapy for patients with eating disorders: A two-site trial with 60-week follow-up. *American Journal of Psychiatry, 166*, 311-319.

[19] Pike, K. M., Walsh, B. T., Vitousek, K., Wilson, G. T., & Bauer, J. (2003). Cognitive behavior therapy in the posthospitalization treatment of anorexia nervosa. *American Journal of Psychiatry*, *160*, 2046-2049.

[20] McIntosh, V.V., Jordan, J., Carter, F.A., Luty, S.E., McKenzie, J.M., Bulik, C.M., Frampton, C.M., & Joyce, P.R. (2005). Three psychotherapies for anorexia nervosa: a randomized, controlled trial. *American Journal of Psychiatry, 162*, 741-747.

[21] Fichter, M. M., & Quadflieg, N. (2007). Long-term stability of eating disorder diagnoses. *International Journal of Eating Disorders, 40 Suppl*, S61-6.

[22] Eddy, K. T., Swanson, S. A., Crosby, R. D., Franko, D. L., Engel, S., Herzog, D. B. (2010) How should DSM-V classify eating disorder not

otherwise specified (EDNOS) presentations in women with lifetime anorexia or bulimia nervosa? *Psychological Medicine*, *40*, 1735-44.

[23] Eddy, K. T., Dorer, D. J., Franko, D. L., Tahilani, K., Thompson-Brenner, H., & Herzog, D. B. (2007). Should bulimia nervosa be subtyped by history of anorexia nervosa? A longitudinal validation. *International Journal of Eating Disorders, 40 Suppl*, S67-71.

[24] First, M., Spitzer, R., Gibbon, M., Williams, J. (1997). *The structured clinical interview for DSM-IV Axis I Disorders, Research Version, Patient Edition, with Psychotic Screen.* New York State Psychiatric Institute, New York.

[25] Fichter, M. M., & Quadflieg, N. (2001). The structured interview for anorexic and bulimic disorders for DSM-IV and ICD-10 (SIAB-EX): Reliability and validity. *European Psychiatry*, 16(1), 38-48.

[26] Keller, M. B., Lavori, P. W., Friedman, B., Nielsen, E., Endicott, J., McDonald-Scott, P., Andreasen, N. C. (1987). The Longitudinal Interval Follow-Up Evaluation : a comprehensive interview for assessing outcome in prospective longitudinal studies. *Archives of General Psychiatry 44*, 540–548.

[27] Garner, D. M., and Garfinkel, P. E. *Handbook of Treatment for Eating Disorders*. New York: Guilford, 1997.

[28] Hagan, M. M., Wauford, P. K., Chandler, P. C., Jarrett, L. A., Rybak, R. J., & Blackburn, K. (2002). A new animal model of binge eating: Key synergistic role of past caloric restriction and stress. *Physiology & Behavior, 77*(1), 45-54.

[29] Muraven, M., Tice, D. M., & Baumeister, R. F. (1998). Self-control as limited resource: Regulatory depletion patterns. *Journal of Personality and Social Psychology, 74*(3), 774-789.

[30] Vohs, K. D., & Heatherton, T. F. (2000). Self-regulatory failure: A resource-depletion approach. *Psychological Science, 11*(3), 249-254.

[31] Cloninger, C. R., Pryzbeck, T. R., Svrakic, D. M., Wetyel, R. D. *TCI The Temperament and Character Inventory (TCI): A Guide to Its Development and Use, Center for Psychobiology of Personality*. St. Louis, Missouri: Washington University, 1994.

[32] DaCosta, M., & Halmi, K. A. (1992). Classifications of anorexia nervosa: Question of subtypes. *International Journal of Eating Disorders, 11,* 305 313.

[33] Mehler, P. S. & Andersen, A. E. (2010). Eating disorders: A guide to medical care and complications. Baltimore: Johns Hopkins University Press.

[34] Fairburn, C. G., Cooper, Z., & O'Connor, M. (2008). Eating Disorders Examination (edition 16.0). In (Fairburn, C. G.) Cognitive Behavior Therapy and Eating Disorders. Guilford: New York.
[35] Serpell, L., & Treasure, J. (2002). Bulimia nervosa: Friend or foe? The pros and cons of bulimia nervosa. *International Journal of Eating Disorders, 32,* 164-170.
[36] First, M. B., Pincus, H. A., Levine, J. B., Williams, J. B., Ustun, B., Peele, R. (2004.) Clinical utility as a criterion for revising psychiatric diagnoses. *American Journal of Psychiatry 161*, 946-954
[37] Arcelus, J., Mitchell, A. J., Wales, J., & Nielsen, S. (2011). Mortality rates in patients with anorexia nervosa and other eating disorders: A meta-analysis of 36 studies. *Archives of General Psychiatry, 68,* 724-731.
[38] Delinsky, S. S., Thomas, J. J., St. Germain, S. A., Weigel, T. J., Levendusky, P. G., & Becker, A. E. (2011). Motivation to change among residential treatment patients with an eating disorder: Assessment of multi-dimensionality of motivation and its relation to treatment outcome. *International Journal of Eating Disorders, 44,* 340-348.
[39] Geller, J., Drab-Hudson, D. L., Whisenhunt, B. L., & Srikameswaran, S. (2004). Readiness to change dietary restriction predicts outcomes in the eating disorders. *Eating Disorders, 12*, 209-224.
[40] Knapp, C. (2003). *Appetites: Why women want.* Berkeley, CA: Counterpoint Press.
[41] Fairburn, C. G. (1995). *Overcoming binge eating.* New York: Guilford
[42] Waller, G., Cordery, H., Corstorphine, E., Hinrichsen, H., Lawson, R., Mountford, V., & Russell, K. (2007*). Cognitive behavioral therapy for eating disorders: A comprehensive treatment guide.* New York: Cambridge University Press.
[43] Hornbacher, M. (1998). *Wasted: a memoir of anorexia and bulimia.* New York: Harper Collins.
[44] Fairburn, C. G. (2008). *Cognitive behavior therapy and eating disorders.* New York: Guilford Press.
[45] Fairburn, C. G., Cooper, Z., & Shafran, R. (2003). Cognitive behaviour therapy for eating disorders: A 'transdiagnostic' theory and treatment. *Behaviour Research and Therapy, 41,* 509-528.
[46] Keski-Rahkonen, A. & Tozzi, F. (2005). The process of recovery in eating disorder sufferers' own words: An internet-based study. *International Journal of Eating Disorders, 37, Suppl.,* S80-S86.

[47] American Psychiatric Association: DSM-5 development. (n.d.) Retrieved from *www.dsm5.org.*

[48] Crow, S. J., Swanson, S. S., Peterson, C. B., Crosby, R. D., Wonderlich, S. A., & Mitchell, J. E. (2011). Latent structure analyses of eating disorder diagnoses. In *Developing an evidence-based classification of eating disorders: scientific findings for DSM-5.* R.H. Striegel-Moore, S.A. Wonderlich, B.T. Walsh, & J.E. Mitchell (Eds), pp. 103-120. Arlington, VA: American Psychiatric Association.

[49] Cain, A. S., Epler, A. J., Steiley, D., & Sher, K. J. (2010). Stability and change in patterns of concerns related to eating, weight, and shape in young adult women: a latent transition analysis. *Journal of Abnormal Psychology, 119*, 255-267.

[50] Lavender, J. M., De Young, K. P., Franko, D. L., Eddy, K. T., Kass, A. E., Sears, M. S., & Herzog, D. B. (In press). An investigation of the joint longitudinal trajectories of low body weight, binge eating, and purging in women with anorexia nervosa and bulimia nervosa. *International Journal of Eating Disorders.*

[51] Sysko, R., Hildebrandt, T., Wilson, G. T., Wilfley, D. E., & Agras, W. S. (2010). Heterogeneity moderates treatment response among patients with binge eating disorder. *Journal of Consulting and Clinical Psychology, 78*, 681-690.

[52] National Institutes of Mental Health (2011). Retrieved from *http://www.nimh.nih.gov/research-funding/rdoc/index.shtml*

[53] Chavez, M., & Insel, T. R. (2007). Eating disorders: National Institute of Mental Health's perspective. *The American Psychologist, 62*, 159-166.

[54] Kaye, W. (2008). Neurobiology of anorexia and bulimia nervosa. *Physiology & Behavior, 94*, 121-135.

[55] Bulik, C. M., Hebebrand, J., Keski-Rahkonen, A., Klump, K. L., Reichborn-Kiennerud, T., Mazzeo, S. E., & Wade, T. D. (2007). Genetic epidemiology, endophenotypes, and classification of eating disorders. *International Journal of Eating Disorders, 40S*, S52-S60.

[56] Bardone-Cone, A. M., Harney, M. B., Maldonado, C. R., Lawson, M. A., Robinson, D. P., Smith, R., & Tosh, A. (2010). Defining recovery from an eating disorder: conceptualization, validation, and examination of psychosocial functioning and psychiatric comorbidity. *Behaviour Research and Therapy, 48*, 194-202.

[57] Couturier, J., & Lock, J. (2006). What is recovery in adolescent anorexia nervosa? *International Journal of Eating Disorders, 39*, 550-555.

In: Anorexia Nervosa
Editor: N. C. Barbarich-Marsteller

ISBN: 978-1-62081-291-4

Chapter 2

A Taxometric Analysis of Anorexia Nervosa

***David H. Gleaves*[*a] *and Alicia C. Snow*[b]**
[a]University of South Australia, Adeleide, SA, Australia
[b]Texas A&M University, College Station, TX, US

Abstract

To examine the latent structure of anorexia nervosa, restricting type, we applied three taxometric procedures (MAMBAC, MAXEIG, and LMODE) to a sample of n = 196 anorexic women and n = 1092 female undergraduate students. Indicators for anorexia nervosa were body mass index and items taken from the Eating Attitudes Test-26. In analyses usinga mixed sample, the results were consistently suggestive of a latent taxon for anorexia nervosa. However, in the undergraduate sample, results were less conclusive and more consistent with a dimensional model suggesting that the findings from the mixed sample may have been artifactual. The findings have implications for etiological models of eating disorders, for assessment of anorexia nervosa and for future taxometric research on anorexia nervosa or other eating disorders.

* Address correspondence to: David H. Gleaves, Ph.D., School of Psychology, Social Work and Social Policy, University of South Australia, Magill Campus, GPO Box 2471, Adelaide, SA 5001, Australia, Email: david.gleaves@unisa.edu.au.

INTRODUCTION

According to the current *Diagnostic and Statistical Manual of Mental Disorders* (DSM-IV-TR; [1]), anorexia nervosais an eating disorder characterized by a refusal to maintain a minimal body weight, an intense fear of gaining weight, and a disturbance in the perception of body shape or size. There are two types, restricting and binge eating/purging, based on the presence or absence of binge eating or purging. The average prevalence of anorexia nervosa is 0.3% among young women [2].

Currently, there is debate over whether eating disorders, including anorexia nervosa, are quantitatively or qualitatively different from normative dieting behavior and weight concerns. That is, do eating disorders represent discrete entities (taxa) [3] or do they fall along one or more continua[4,5] from normal body weight and eating concerns to severely disturbed patterns of eating (see 6,7,8 for reviews of eating disorder research in this area). The question of taxonicity regarding anorexia nervosa is important for several reasons. If anorexic eating attitudes and behaviors are discovered to be taxonic, this would hold implications for etiology, assessment, prevention, treatment, and research. For instance, if a taxon for anorexic eating attitudes and behaviors was known, highly valid and efficient screening measures could be devised to identify individuals at greater risk for developing anorexia nervosa. This would allow prevention efforts to be focused on the high-risk group. If, on the other hand, anorexic eating attitudes and behaviors are found to occur along a continuum, from normal to disordered eating, preventative efforts would need to be widely disseminated.

The issue of continuity versus discontinuity is also not unique to the eating disorders.Personality theorists have debated for decades about whether or not personality can be placed on a continuum from normal to abnormal [9],and discussions regarding the *Diagnostic and Statistical Manual of Mental Disorders* often center on whether it should be based on categorical or dimensional classification schemes [10]. The most recent version is attempting to incurporate both in some instances (i.e., personality disorders).

Taxometric Research Methods

Although a variety of methods have been tried to determine if a construct is dimensional or taxonic (see [6] or [7] for research in the context of eating disorders), the most sound methods are the taxometric procedures developed by Meehl and colleagues [11, 12]. These procedures, including Maximum Covariance (MAXCOV; [13]), Mean above minus below a cut (MAMBAC; [14]), and Latent Mode factor analysis (L-Mode; [12]) were developed specifically to detect the existence of latent class variables, or taxa.They allow the data to determine whether or not a taxonic model is appropriate. Numerous Monte Carlo investigations have demonstrated that discrete and continuous latent variables can indeed be distinguished quite reliably using taxometric procedures [12, 15, 16] and these methods have now been applied to a large number of personality or psychopathology constructs (see [15] or [16] for reviews).

Previous Taxometric Work with Eating Disorders

Currently, there are no large scale published taxometric studies of anorexia nervosa. Published research has predominantly either focused on bulimia nervosa or anorexia nervosa as it relates to bulimia nervosa, or on eating disorder symptomatology rather than eating disorders per se [17]. In a study of bulimia nervosa, Gleaves, Lowe, Snow, Green, and Murphy-Eberenz [18] used two taxometric procedures (MAXCOV and MAMBAC) with clinical (n = 201) and non-clinical (n = 412) samples. Indicators were items from the BULIMA Test- Revised [19] and the Eating Attitudes Test-26 [20]. The authors first analyzed a 50/50 mixed sample (using only a subset of the non-clinical data), and results suggested the existence of a latent taxon underlying bulimia nervosa. To rule out the possibility that the results were merely artifactual (the result of analyzing an aggregate sample), the authors then analyzed the sample of undergraduate women alone. The authors predicted that, if bulimia nervosa was taxonic, analysis of this second sample would also reveal taxonicity, but that the shape of the resultant functions would reflect a low baserate taxon. Results were indeed suggestive of a low base rate taxon.

Williamson et al., [21] studied women that were either eating disordered (n = 201), obese (n = 24), or normal-weight non-eating disordered (n = 116). Eating disordered participants were diagnosed as having: bulimia nervosa, purging type (n = 38); bulimia nervosa, non-purging type (n = 7); anorexia nervosa, restricting type (n = 19); anorexia nervosa, binge-eating/purging type (n = 16); eating disorder not otherwise specified, other than binge eating disorder (n = 78); or binge eating disorder (n = 43). Among other analyses, the authors compared each eating disorder diagnosis with an appropriate control group to see whether each is best conceptualized as different in degree or kind from the respective control groups. The authors concluded that all of the diagnoses except anorexia nervosa appeared taxonic, with results being mixed (i.e., two plots each suggesting taxonicity and dimensionality, with two more rated as ambiguous) for anorexia nervosa. However, the sample size was inadequate to draw definitive conclusions regarding anorexia.

Using a larger clinical sample of 745 eating disordered women (along with 214 non-clinical undergraduate students), Gleaves, Lowe, Green, Cororve, and Williams [22] usedtwo taxometric procedures (MAMBAC and MAXCOV; see below) to more closely examine the question of whether the various eating disorder diagnoses are qualitatively different from one another. The clinical participants were diagnosed, based on archival semi-structured interview data and DSM-IV criteria, with either anorexia nervosa, restricting type (n = 70); anorexia nervosa, binge-eating/purging type (n = 95); bulimia nervosa, purging type (n = 514); bulimia nervosa, non-purging type (n = 48); or eating disorder not otherwise specified (EDNOS; n = 18).

Gleaves, Lowe, Green et al., [22] conducted a series of analyses, some of which are particularly relevant here. One set of analysis compared anorexia nervosa and bulimia nervosa, collapsing both across their subtypes. Results were mixed for both taxometric procedures, with some appearing taxonic whereas others appeared dimensional, a result that was not surprising considering that the groups were mixtures of subtypes. Another analysis compared bingeing and non-bingeing forms of eating disorders. The bingeing group comprised three diagnoses: anorexia nervosa, binge-eating/purging type and bulimia nervosa, both purging and non-purging types. The non-bingeing group comprised persons diagnosed with anorexia nervosa, restricting subtype. Results were suggestive of taxonicity, suggesting that eating disorders characterized by binge eating are qualitatively different from those without binge eating.

The fifth analysis separately compared the purging and non-purging subtypes of bulimia nervosa with anorexia nervosa, binge-eating/purging type. For the bulimia nervosa, purging type versus anorexia nervosa, binge-eating/purging type, only one variable (BMI) differentiated these two groups by at least one standard deviation. Thus taxometric analyses, which require at least two indicators, could not be performed. The finding that these two disorders were not even able to pass the first of a multiple-hurdles, multiple-consistency test of taxonicity provided some evidence of dimensionality. There were only two variables that differentiated the bulimia nervosa, non-purging group from the binge-eating/purging anorexia nervosa group, and the resultant graphs were indicative of dimensionality.

The next two analyses compared anorexia nervosa, restricting type with the purging and non-purging subtypes of bulimia nervosa. The results were suggestive of a latent taxon that differentiated the two subtypes of bulimia nervosa from the restricting subtype of anorexia nervosa. In the ninth analysis, the two anorexia nervosa subtypes (i.e., restricting and binge-eating/purging types) were compared, and the results suggested a latent taxon.

To summarize, the two subtypes of anorexia nervosa were found to be qualitatively distinct, with anorexia nervosa, binge-eating/purging type falling along a continuum with both subtypes of bulimia nervosa. It appears that anorexia nervosa, binge-eating/purging type is more qualitatively distinct from anorexia nervosa, restricting type than it is from either subtype of bulimia nervosa, calling to question the current DSM-IV (and proposed DSM-V) classification of these disorders.However, because the non-clinical group was relatively small (n = 214), and because such composite samples are not ideal for taxometric analyses, the authors were not able to adequately test the continuity of anorexia nervosa with normality.

There have been more recent taxometric studies related to eating disorders but none have definitely tested the taxonicity of anorexia nervosa.Tylka and Subich [23] applied two taxometric methods (MAXCOV and L-Mode,) to a sample of 532 female college students. The authors chose “nonbehavioral” (p. 276) indicators such as body dissatisfaction, neuroticism, and poor interoceptive awareness, and found results indicative of dimensionality. However, because their indicators were broad and not specifically indicative of eating disorders (particularly any specific type of eating disorder), it is difficult to know what if anything can be concluded from the results.

Most recently, Holm-Denoma, Richey, and Joiner [17] examined the latent structure of dietary restraint, body dissatisfaction, and drive for thinness using MAMBAC and MAXCOV with a fairly large sample of 2,836 women in total, and concluded that each of the constructs had a dimensional latent structure. In contrast with Tylka and Subich [23], Holm-Donoma et al, did not claim to be studying the taxonicity of eating disorders per se but rather “theoretically relevant variables that have been shown to cut across eating disorder diagnoses” (p. 788). Although interesting and potentially meaningful on their own, their results do not address the question of whether or not anorexia nervosa is taxonic or dimensional.In fact, according to Meehl [3], the question of whether a taxon is involved in a pattern of relationships is often confused by the widespread ambiguous definition of a category or class concept. A category or class has often been misrepresented as necessarily involving sharp distinctions or clear-cut boundaries. This notion involves confusion between indicators and the latent taxon they indicate. For example, if a taxon is involved in eating disorders, individuals may either possess or not possess the latent taxon, but if they do possess it, the indicators of the taxon (e.g.,eating disorder symptoms) may be either qualitative or quantitative in nature. Weight and/or number of binge eating episodes per week may be examples of quantitative indicators, whereas the theoretical assumption that weight loss represents the arena where a subset of psychologically vulnerable persons struggle to gain autonomy and competence (i.e., Bruch, [24]) may refer to a qualitative indicator. In other words, there should be clear-cut boundaries where the taxa are concerned. Individuals either possess the taxon or they do not. Clear cut boundaries may or may not exist among the indicators of a taxon [3].Therefore, the fact that eating disorder symptoms such as dieting or degree of weight loss seem to be continuously distributed does not disqualify the disorder from being taxonic..

From the existing research, it seems clear that further taxometric study of the latent structure of anorexia nervosa is warranted and that two factors need to be present in a methodologically sound taxometric study. First, when clinical data are used, the restricting and bulimic (binge eating/purging) subtypes of anorexia nervosa need to be studied separately. Given the research described above suggesting that bulimic form of anorexia nervosa may occur on a continuum with bulimia nervosa, one could argue that it is the restricting form of anorexia nervosa that needs more research. Second, because of the problem with possible artifactual evidence of taxonicity caused by examination of aggregate samples, it is critical that a large general sample also be examined (some researchers would argue that only large general samples should be used; we address this issue in our discussion). However, because of the low base rate of anorexia nervosa (relative to bulimia nervosa), this sample would need to be sufficiently large (we reasoned at least $N = 1000$).Thus, the purpose of this study was to perform a taxometric analysis of anorexia nervosa using both a mixed sample and a large general sample.

METHOD

Participants

A total of 1313 women participated in the study. The non-clinical sample of 1092 women was from introductory psychology courses at a large University in the United States. Their mean age was 18.79 (*S.D.* = 1.24) and body mass index (BMI; kg/m^2) was 21.83 (*S.D.* = 3.53). The clinical sample consisted of 196 women from a residential eating disorder treatment facility. All were diagnosed, based on a semistructured interview and DSM-III-R [25] or DSM-IV [26] criteria, as having anorexia nervosa (restricting type if with DSM-IV criteria or no current or past bulimia nervosa if using DSM-III-R criteria). They had a mean BMI of 15.97 (*S.D.* = 2.02) and their mean age was 22.39 (*S.D.* = 8.19).

Measures

Indicators for all taxometric analyses were drawn from the Eating Attitudes Test-26 (EAT-26; [20]). The test is a 26-item self-report measure that evaluates behaviors and attitudes characteristic of anorexia nervosa. Each item of the EAT-26 is responded to on a six-point scale.For the present study, the standard scoring system (0,0,0,1,2,3), as well as an alternate scoring system (1,2,3,4,5,6) for the non-clinical sample was employed. The alternate scoring method, by increasing scoring variability, was used to ensure that the standard scoring method did not artificially lead to results suggestive of taxonicity. We also used BMI as an indicator.

Data Analyses: MAMBAC,MAXEIG, and L-Mode Taxometric Methods

The taxometric procedures used were MAMBAC [14], MAXEIG[12] and LMode [12]. Below we describe each of these (although see [15]; and [12] for more detailed discussions).All taxometric analyses were carried out using the R computing environment and Ruscio's source code [25].

MAMBAC. This procedure requires the use of two independent (uncorrelated within groups) indicators at a time, of which one must be continuous, out of a pool of conjectured taxon indicators. The continuous indicator is used as the input variable (x), with the second indicator (y) as the output variable. Successive cuts are made along the input variable, with the mean of the output variable below the cut subtracted from the mean above the cut. These output scores are computed and plotted at every cut along the input variable distribution, resulting in a characteristic mountain-like function if a latent taxon exists. With a .5 base rate taxon, that peak would be in the middle of the graph; with larger or smaller base rates it would shift to the left or right respectively. On the other hand, in the case of a latent dimension, the prototypical MAMBAC curve will have a dish-like shape.

MAXEIG. This second procedure, first described by Waller and Meehl [12] is a multivariate extension of the MAXCOV procedure [13]. One indicator serves as the input and the remaining indicators contribute to the output. All of the remaining indicators are entered in a principal components analysis and the eigenvalue of the first principal component is plotted on the *y*-axis across intervals of the input variable. The eigenvalue thus represents the multivariate analogue of the covariance (as in MAXCOV). Taxonic data will prototypically yield a graph that peaks at the window with the subsample most evenly divided between members of the taxon and complement. With a .5 base rate taxon, that peak would again be in the middle of the graph; with larger or smaller base rates it would shift to the left or right respectively. Dimensional graphs would typically be relatively flat.

The L-MODE taxometric procedure [12] uses factor analysis to evaluate latent structure. Again graphs are utilized, in this case the distribution of cases' estimated scores on a single latent factor are plotted. The estimated scores are calculated by factor analysis constrained to a one-factor solution. A bimodal distribution of factors scores is indicative of taxonic structure, whereas unimodal distribution suggests a dimensional structure of the latent variable [12].

Above we have described the appearance of prototypical taxonic or dimensional plots. However, when data are non-normal, plots do not always take the characteristic form. In such situations, distinguishing between taxonic and dimensional data is more difficult. Some researchers [15, 18] have found it useful to simulate dimensional or taxonic datasets that match the distributional characteristics of the research data. Taxometric results based on those datasets can then be compared with those from the research data to determine which are more similar. Ruscio and colleagues have also developed an index of the extent to which results for the research data are more similar to the taxonic or dimensional comparison data. Their Comparison Curve Fit Index (CCFI) ranges from 0 (consistent with dimensional structure) to 1 (consistent with taxonic structure). When $.40 < \text{CCFI} < .60$, it should be interpreted with caution. There is evidence that CCFI values can discriminate between taxonic and dimensional data across a range of data conditions [28], particularly when the CCFI from different procedures agree.As noted, all taxometric analyses were conducted using the R statistical package and programs written by

Ruscio [27] and included generation of comparsion taxonic and dimensional data and the CCFI.

RESULTS

Taxometric Analyses aithaMixed Sample

To facilitate taxometric plot interpretation, and to pick the best indicators, we first examined a mixed sample with the 196women from the anorexia nervosa sample and a matching number from the college sample (randomly selected from the total). We used an empirical approach to selecting indicators. To eliminate poor indicators, items with standard deviation differences (Cohen's *d* values, anorexia nervosa vs. non-clinical) of less than 1.25, and those with low correlations with the overall scale (based on the total sample) were removed. This process left us with six items: 2 ("Avoid eating when I am hungry"), 3 ("Find myself preoccupied with food"), 8 ("Feel that others would prefer if I ate more", 18 ("Feel that food controls my life"), 21 ("Give too much time and thought to food"), and 24 ("Like my stomach to be empty"). To reduce redundancy (and subsequent nuisance covariance), we then aggregated variables with substantial inter-group correlations. This process left us with three variables from the EAT-26; aggregate1 (item 3 + item 18 + item 21), aggregate2 (item 2 + item 24), and variable 8. Our fourth indicator was BMI, which also showed good validity (Cohen's $d = 2.09$).

We first conducted MAMBAC analyses on the four resulting indicators. However, it is important to note that use of BMI as an indicator [of anorexia nervosa] in MAMBAC required that it be reverse scored (multiplied by -1 or transformed in some other way). That is, the more "anorexic" someone is, the less her BMI, whereas the items from the EAT-26 are positively associated with anorexia nervosa. Failure to account for this scoring issue would lead to the MAMBAC graphs resembling a mirror image of the actual graph. In other words, taxonic graphs would look dimensional and vice-versa.

In the MAMBAC analyses, all four indicators continued to show good validity (based on estimated taxon and complement grouping) with an average Cohen's $d = 2.5$. The set of 12 MAMBAC plots all clearly looked taxonic with the characteristic mountain shape consistent with a mid-range base rate. Base rate estimates were in fact .47 for the average of each indicator and .48 for the average curve. Average plots compared with simulated taxonic and dimensional data are presented in Figure 1. For this and all figures, the dark dotted line is based on the research data. The grey lines represent the middle 50% of simulated data and the lightest lines show the maximum and minimum values. The CCFI was .90 which is strongly suggestive of taxonicity.

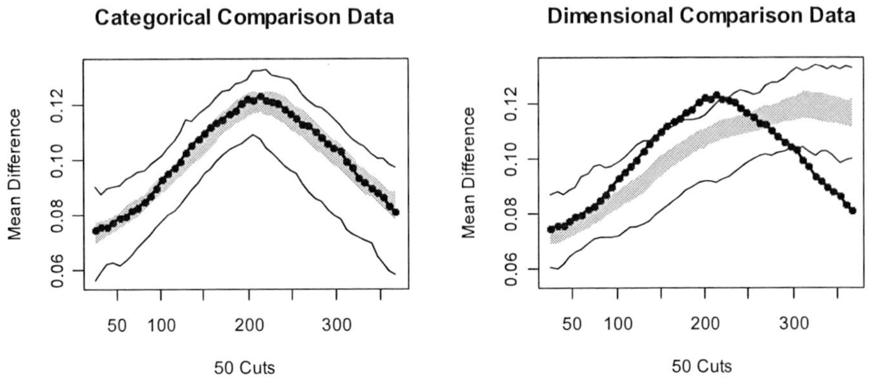

Figure 1. Averaged MAMBAC Graph based on Mixed Sample Analyses.

For the MAXEIG analyses with the mixed sample,all four indicators continued to show good validity (average Cohen's d = 2.5). The four MAXEIG graphs also looked clearly taxonic and suggestive of a mid range base rate. Actual base rate estimates were .48 for the average of each indicator and for the average graph. The average in comparison with the simulated taxonic and dimensional data is depicted in Figure 2.The CCFI was .95 which is strongly indicative of taxonicity.

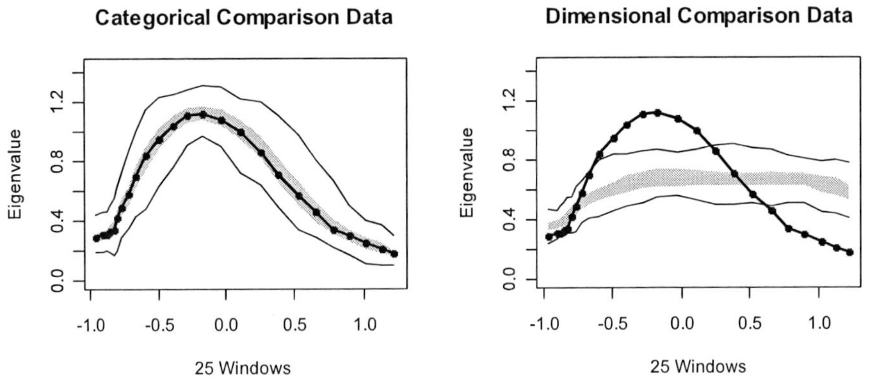

Figure 2. Averaged MAXEIG Graph based on Mixed Sample Analyses.

For the LMode analyses, indicators again showed a very good average validity of $d = 2.5$. The LMode procedure only generates one graph and, in this case, it had a clear bimodal pattern indicative of taxonicity. The figure, along with comparison taxonic and dimensional graphs is presented in Figure. 3. The CCFI was .91 which is again strongly indicative of taxonicity.

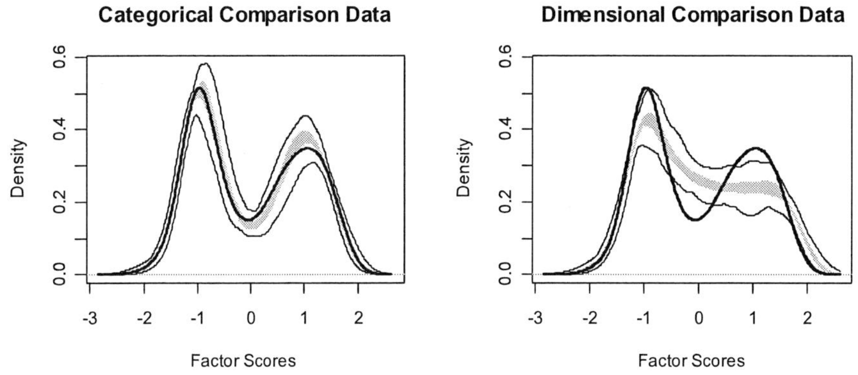

Figure 3. L-Mode Graphs based on Analyses with Mixed Sample.

In summary, all of the analyses with the mixed sample yielded results that suggested the presence of a latent taxon. However many researchers suggest that such situations may give rise to false taxa or “pseudotaxa”. For that reason, we subsequently analyzed the large college student sample. We reasoned that, if anorexia nervosa is taxonic, then the results would also be suggestive of a taxon but with a much lower base rate.

Taxometric Analyses of theCollege-Student Sample

With the college sample we then performed the same three taxometric procedures (MAMBAC, MAXEIG, and LMode). We also conducted two sets of analyses,one using the standard-scored (0-3) EAT-26 data and a second using an alternate-scored (1-6) data. We were not able to re-score the clinical data using the 1-6 format because the dataset was archival.

For MAMBAC with the standard scored data, validity estimates were lower than those from earlier analyses (average d = 1.31). Although the indicators from the EAT-26 ranged from d = 1.36 to d = 1.78, the validity estimate for BMI was only d = 0.47. Average MAMBAC graphs, along with those from simulated comparison data, are presented in Figure 4. As can be seen, the task of determining if the results based on the research data are more similar to those from the simulated taxonic versus dimensional data was much more difficult than in the first set of analysis. In fact, the CCFI was 0.44 which is in the range suggesting that it should be interpreted with caution. The results based on the simulated taxonic data, however, did have a cusp toward the right boundary which was not evident in the results based on the simulated dimensional data or the research data. Thus the result is more consistent with a dimensional interpretation. Base rate estimates averaged across indicators and for the average graph were 0.236 and 0.117 respectively.

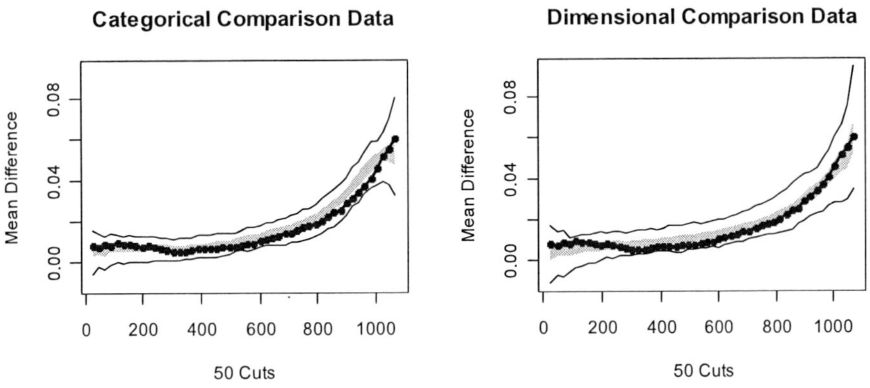

Figure 4. Averaged MAMBAC Graphs with College Sample and Traditional Scoring of EAT-26.

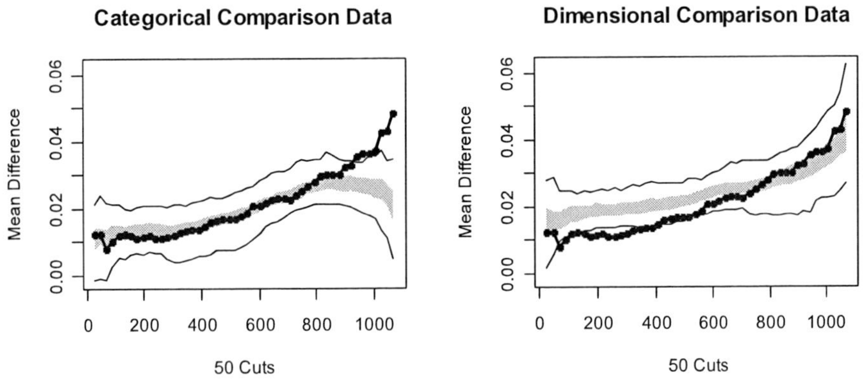

Figure 5. Averaged MAMBAC Graphs with College Sample 1-6 Scoring System.

With the MAMBAC results based on the 1-6 scoring of the EAT-26 items, the same pattern emerged and it was more evident. That is, the cusps toward the right boundary of the simulated taxonic graph were more evident and there was no such cusp in the graphs based on the research data.However, the CCFI was again 0.44 suggesting that the comparisons with the simulated taxonic and dimensional data are not obvious. It is noteworthy also that the validity estimates for the indicators were again lower than they were with the separate groups analysis. The average Cohen's *d* was 1.10 and the validity estimate was again lower for BMI ($d = 0.58$). Base rate estimates averaged across indicators and for the average graph were 0.43 and 0.20 respectively. The lack of consistency in base rate estimation may be a further indication of dimensionality. That is, the base rate of a taxon cannot be reliably estimated because it (the taxon) does not exist.

For MAXEIG and the standard scoring, the overall pattern of results was similar to those from MAMBAC. Base rate estimates averaged across indicators and for the average graph were 0.21 and 0.19 respectively. The average indicator validity was $d = 1.40$ but validity was again lower for BMI ($d = 0.48$). The graphs (see Figure 6) were quite difficult to interpret. As can be seen, graphs based on simulated taxonic and dimensional data were quite similar, and the graphs based on the research data were not obviously more similar to one than the other. The CCFI, however, was 0.38 which is moderately suggestive of dimensionality.

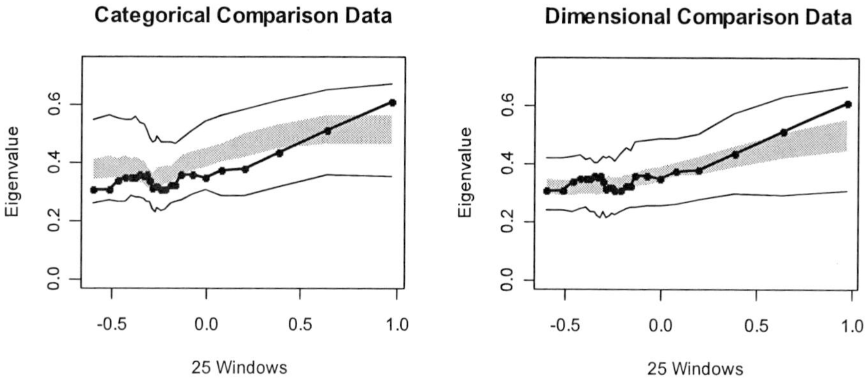

Figure 6. Averaged MAXEIG Graph with College Sample Traditional Scoring.

With MAXEIG and the 1-6 scoring, validity estimates were similar to the previous analysis (average $d = 1.25$ and and $d = 0.55$ for BMI). Base rate estimates averaged across indicators and for the average curve were 0.26 and 0.23 respectively. At least based on visual inspection (see Figure 7), graphs were more consistent with a dimensional interpretation. Graphs based on the simulated taxonic data demonstrated a cusp toward the right boundary which was not evident in the graphs from the research data. However, the CCFI was = 0.55 which is in the "interpret with caution" range.

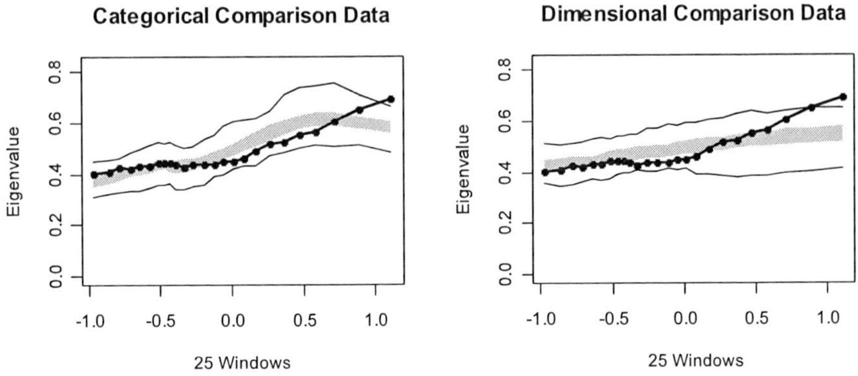

Figure 7. Averaged MAXEIG Graph with College Sample, Alternative scoring.

Finally, when we applied LMode to the college sample using the standard scoring, a somewhat different pattern emerged for some of the results. The average validity estimate was d = 1.81 and the estimate for BMI was 0.60. Base rate estimates were 0.23 when based on location of left mode and 0.50 when based on location of right. The LMode graph was quite difficult to interpret and did not look obviously like either the taxonic or dimensional graphs (see Figure 8). However, the CCFI was 0.38 which is moderate evidence of dimensionality.

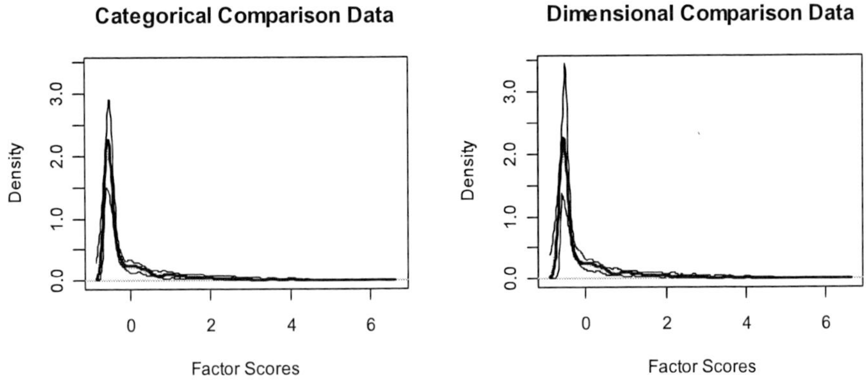

Figure 8. L-Mode Graphs with College Sample and Traditional Scoring.

When we applied LMode to the dataset based on 1-6 scoring of the EAT-26, indicator validity estimates had an average of d = 1.55and the estimate for BMI was d = 0.62. The base rate estimate based on location of left mode was 0.32 and 0.49 based on location of the right. The graphs were not obviously indicative of taxonicity or dimensionality, although the CCFI was 0.39 which is mild evidence of dimensionality.

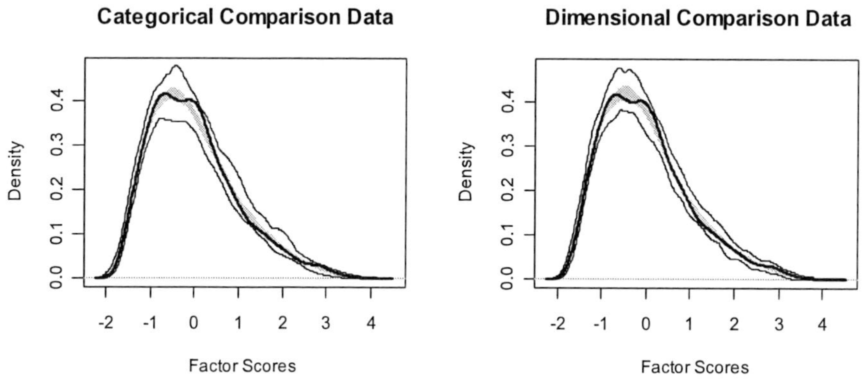

Figure 9. L-Mode Graphs with College Sample and Alternative Scoring

DISCUSSION

Results of the mixed sample analyseswere consistently indicative of a taxon underlying anorexia nervosa. The graphs all displayed the characteristic shape of taxonic data, and the CCFI values were consistently indicative of a taxon. Furthermore, the base rate estimates were consistent with the known group membership, although we would have predicted an estimate slightly higher (rather than lower) than .5 if all those in the anorexia nervosa group were taxon members and a small number of the college sample were. Overall, it seems clear that the taxometric methods consistently detected something. The question is whether it was a genuine taxon or a pseudo taxon created by the sampling or measurement strategy.

Results with the large college sample suggest it was probably the latter as they looked quite a bit different from those with the mixed sample. Individual graphs rarely if ever were indicative of a taxon. Averaged graphs, which are presented in the figures, were either ambiguous or indicative of dimensionality. If anything, this pattern was clearer when the continuous 1-6 scoring was used than when the traditional scoring was used. We were unfortunately unable to examine the continuous scoring with the clinical dataset so were unable to determine if those results may have looked more dimensional with the 1-6 scoring.

Taken as a whole and considering the known limitations of using mixed samples, we would argue that the results are more consistent with a dimensional model of anorexia nervosa, restricting type. Of course, it is possible that the disorder is taxonic, that the taxon was detected with the mixed samples, but that our analysis with the college sample was unable to detect the taxon. There are a variety of reasons why this might be the case, the most compelling being that the sample size was not large enough to detect a small taxon. Although our college sample was reasonably large (n = 1092), anorexia nervosa is a relatively rare condition. A recent review of prevalence studies [2] concluded that it has an average prevalence of .3% among young women. That would, of course, equate to approximately 3 women in our sample which would be very difficult to detect. However, a taxon is not necessarily a disorder per se and, if a taxon is a latent predisposition to develop a disorder under the right (or wrong) circumstances (as was described in much of the early work of Paul Meehl) then we would expect a prevalence that is considerably higher than the actual rate of the disorder. If this was the case, then our sample size should have been adequate. The base rate estimates, however, were unexpectedly high and generally over .20. Clearly, whatever was being detected was not anorexia nervosa per se, and the variability in base rate estimates would further challenge the possibility of a taxon being detected.

It is also noteworthy that the validity of BMI as an indicator was generally poor for these analyses. This finding would suggest that the subgroup of women being identified was not necessarily low weight. The content of the six EAT-26 items tells us a bit more about them. The items were:2 ("Avoid eating when I am hungry"), 3 ("Find myself preoccupied with food"), 8 ("Feel that others would prefer if I ate more"), 18 ("Feel that food controls my life"), 21 ("Give too much time and thought to food"), and 24 ("Like my stomach to be empty"). The group identified may in fact be the "weight preoccupied" women that have been identified in previous research [29].

We should comment further on the issue of indicator validity so that there is no confusion. We reported that we initially selected only those indicators with the highest validity defined as separation of the anorexia nervosa and comparison group. When reporting results, however, we also reported item validities generated from the analysis. These differed from the original ones because they were based on taxon and complement membership estimated from the program. Specifically, cases are first classified using the mean base rate estimate. Then those with the highest total scores on all indicators are assigned to the taxon group and the remainder to the complement group. Indicator validity is then calculated based on those group assignments which are, of course, not necessarily accurate. Furthermore, if a construct is dimensional, there is no taxon or complement group. In our analyses with the mixed sample, the base rate estimates were generally close to the actual group membership, and the validity estimates were similar to those based on the known group composition. It was with the college sample that the estimates varied.

It is also noteworthy that our analyses were limited to the items of the EAT-26, which are pretty much limited to eating related behaviours and attitudes. It is possible that if psychopathology was more broadly measured, including constructs such as ineffectiveness, interoceptive awareness, and interpersonal distrust, we might have found different results [29].The items from the EAT-26, however, were generated specifically to measure the symptoms of anorexia nervosa.

It is also important to note that these results do not address the question of whether or not the distinction between restricting anorexia nervosa and the binge-eating purging sub-type is taxonic or dimensional because we did not study the latter. The earlier study by Gleaves, Lowe, Green et al. [22] found that the distinction between those two sub-types appeared taxonic whereas the distinction between the two subtypes of BN appeared dimensional.

An additional limitation of the analysis of the mixed sample is that alternate scoring data for the clinical sample was not available (because the data were archival and hard copies were not obtainable), and thus the possibility of artificial taxonicity due to standard scoring procedures could not be further examined. There are thus two possible reasons why the results with the mixed sample may be indicative of a pseudotaxon rather than a genuine. One reason is the nature of the scale used and the second is the composition of the sample.

On the topic of composite samples, given the criticisms that some researchers [15, 16] put forward regarding their use, one might ask if there is any benefit in using them at all. We would suggest that there are at least two. The first is that it allows for more accurate measurement of indicator validity. Methods such as that used by Rucio's programs (as described above) produce an indexof validity, defined as the separation in SD units between a taxon and complement group *even if a sample is dimensional,* which is of course contradictory.Had we, in fact, only used the college sample, our validity estimates would have been off; BMI was not even identified as a valid indicator in those analyses, although it is obvious that it should be an indicator of anorexia nervosa.The second possible benefit of using combined samples is that such samples do not always yield results indicative of taxonicity [22, 30]. Thus, if such a sampling approach is used and there is still evidence of dimensionality, we would consider that fairly strong evidence of dimensionality. We would not, however, recommend using combined samples in isolation but rather at a first step in a series of analyses as we have done here and elsewhere [22].

CONCLUSION

Our results, although not without limitations, are most consistent with a dimensional model of anorexia nervosa, restricting type, suggesting that it may occur on a continuum with milder forms of eating disturbance and normative dieting and weight concerns. The results also illustrate some of the complexities of doing taxometric research with real data. Future research should attempt to study the question with an even larger sample and a potentially wider range of indicators. If mixed samples are used, a larger general population sample needs to be used also.

ACKNOWLEDGMENTS

This chapter was partially based on the doctoral dissertation of the second author while she was at Texas A&M University. Clinical data were collected while the first author was a Research Associate at The Renfrew Foundation, Philadelphia, PA.The project described was partially supported by Grant Number R03 MH064599-02 from the National Institute of Mental Health (NIMH). Its contents are solely the responsibility of the authors and do not necessarily represent the official views of the NIMH.

REFERENCES

[1] American Psychiatric Association. (2000). *Diagnostic and statistical manual of mental disorders (4th ed-Text Revision).* Washington, DC: Author.

[2] Hoek, H. W., & Van Hoeken, D. (2003). Review of the prevalence and incidence of eating disorders. *International Journal of Eating Disorders*, 34, 383-396.

[3] Meehl, P. E. (1995). Bootstraps taxometrics:Solving the classification problem in psychopathology.*American Psychologist*, 50, 266-275.

[4] Scarano, G. M., & Kalodner-Martin, C. R. (1994). A description of the continuum of eating disorders: Implications for intervention and research. *Journal of Counseling & Development,* 72, 356-361.

[5] Tylka, T. L., & Subich, L. M. (1999). Exploring the construct validity of the eating disorder continuum. *Journal of Counseling Psychology*, 46, 268–276.

[6] Gleaves, D. H., Brown, J. D., & Warren, C. S. (2004). The continuity/discontinuity models of eating disorders: A review of the literature and implications for assessment, treatment, and prevention. *Behavior Modification*, 28, 739-762.

[7] Williamson, D. A., Gleaves, D. H., & Stewart, T. (2005). Categorical versus dimensional models of eating disorders: An examination of the Evidence. *International Journal of Eating Disorders,* 37, 1-10.

[8] Wonderlich, S., Joiner, T., Keel, P., Williamson, D., & Crosby, R. (2007). Eating disorder diagnoses: Empirical approaches to classification. *American Psychologist,* 62, 167–180.

[9] Allport, G. W. (1950). *The nature of personality: Selected papers.* Cambridge, MA: Addison Wesley.

[10] Widiger, T. A., & Mullins-Sweatt, S. (2007). Mental disorders as discrete clinical conditions: Dimensional versus categorical classification. In M. Hersen, S. M. Turner, & D. C. Beidel (Eds.). *Adult psychopathology and diagnosis* (pp. 3-33). Hoboken, NJ: Wiley.

[11] Meehl, P. E., & Golden, R. R. (1982). Taxometric methods. In P. Kendall & J. butcher (Eds.), *Handbook of research methods in clinical psychology* (pp. 127 181). New York: Wiley.

[12] Waller, N. G., & Meehl, P. E. (1998). *Multivariate taxometric procedures: Distinguishing types from continua.* Newbury Park: Sage.

[13] Meehl, P. E., & Yonce, L. Y. (1996). Taxometric analysis: II. Detecting taxonicity using covariance of two quantitative indicators in successive intervals of a third indicator (MAXCOV Procedure). *Psychological Reports*, 78 (Monograph sup., 1-v78), 1091-1227.

[14] Meehl, P. E., & Yonce, L. Y. (1994). Taxometric analysis I. Detecting taxonicity with two quantitative indicators using means above and below

a sliding cut (MAMBAC procedure).*Psychological Reports*, 74 (monograph supp.,1-V74), 1059-1274.

[15] Ruscio, J., Haslam, N., & Ruscio, A. M. (2006*). Introduction to the taxometric method: A practical guide*. Mahwah, NJ: Lawrence Erlbaum Associates.

[16] Schmidt, N. B., Kotov, R., & Joiner, T. E. (2004). *Taxometrics: Toward a new diagnostic scheme for psychology*. Washington, DC: American Psychological Association.

[17] Holm-Denoma, J. M., Richey, J. A., & Joiner, T. E. (2010). The latent structure of dietary restraint, body dissatisfaction, and drive for thinness: a series of taxometric analyses. *Psychological Assessment*, 22, 788–797.

[18] Gleaves, D. H., Lowe, M. R., Snow, A. C., Green, B. A., & Murphy-Eberenz, K. P. (2000). The Continuity and discontinuity models of bulimia nervosa: A Taxometric investigation. *Journal of Abnormal Psychology*, 109 56-68.

[19] Thelen, M. H., Farmer, J., Wonderlich, S., & Smith, M. (1991). A revision of the Bulimia Test: The BULIT-R. *Psychological Assessment*, 3, 119-124.

[20] Garner, D. M., Olmsted, M. P., Bohr, Y., & Garfinkel, P. E. (1982). The Eating Attitudes Test: Psychometric features and clinical correlates. *Psychological Medicine,* 12, 871-878.

[21] Williamson, D. A., Womble, L. G., Smeets, M. A. M., Netemeyer, R. G., Thaw, J., Kutlesic, V., & Gleaves, D. H. (2002).The latent structure of eating disorder symptoms: A factor analytic and taxometric investigation. *American Journal of Psychiatry*,159, 412-418.

[22] Gleaves, D. H., Lowe, M. R., Green, B. A., Cororve, M. B., & Williams, T. L. (2000). Do Anorexia and Bulimia Nervosa Occur on a Continuum? *A Taxometric Analysis. Behavior Therapy*, 31, 195-219.

[23] Tylka, T.L., & Subich, L.M. (2003). Revisiting the latent structure of eating disorders: Taxometric analyses with nonbehavioral indicators. *Journal of Counseling Psychology*, 50, 276–286.

[24] Bruch, H. (1973). *Eating Disorders*. New York: Basic Books.

[25] American Psychiatric Association. (1987). *Diagnostic and statistical manual of mental disorders (3rd ed. revised).* Washington, DC: Author.

[26] American Psychiatric Association. (1994). Diagnostic *and statistical manual of mental disorders (4th ed.)*. Washington, DC: Author.

[27] Ruscio, J. (2011). Taxometric program documentation, R language [Computer software andmanual]. Retrieved from *http://www.tcnj.edu/~ruscio/taxometrics.html*.

[28] Ruscio, J., Walters, G. D., Marcus, D. K., & Kaczetow, W. (2010). Comparing the relative fit of categorical and dimensional latent variable models using consistency tests. *Psychological Assessment,* 22, 5-21.

[29] Garner, D. M., Olmsted, M. P., & Garfinkel, P. E. (1983). Does anorexia nervosa occur on a continuum? *International Journal of Eating Disorders*, 2, 11-20.

[30] Haslam, N., & Beck, A. T. (1994). Subtyping major depression: A taxometric analysis. *Journal of Abnormal Psychology*, 103, 686-692.

In: Anorexia Nervosa
Editor: N. C. Barbarich-Marsteller

ISBN: 978-1-62081-291-4

Chapter 3

Physical Activity in Anorexia Nervosa

Diane A. Klein *

Associate Professor of Clinical Psychiatry, Columbia University College of Physicians &Surgeons, The New York State Psychiatric Institute, New York, NY, US

Abstract

Excessive physical activity is often observed in patients with Anorexia Nervosa (AN) and may contribute to significant clinical difficulties. Physical activity may assume a range of forms including pacing, fidgeting and exercise behavior. This chapter will review the manifestations and clinical correlates of excessive physical activity in people with AN, as well as possible treatment implications. The animal model of "Activity Based Anorexia" will be presented in light of its relevance to the clinical phenomenon of excessive physical activity in AN.

* Associate Professor of Clinical Psychiatry, Columbia University College of Physicians &Surgeons, The New York State Psychiatric Institute, 1051 Riverside Drive, Unit 98, New York, NY 10032, T212 543-6807 F212 543-5607, Email dk2127@columbia.edu

Introduction

Physical activity plays an important role in energy regulation and often appears to be excessive among people with Anorexia Nervosa (AN). This chapter presents an overview of the varying manifestations of physical activity in this population, clinical problems it may pose, and approaches used in treatment; selected research topics and future research directions are discussed.

I. Physical Activity in AN: Definition and Clinical Features

Elevated levels of physical activity are commonly observed in patients with AN, to the extent that some consider it a "fundamental clinical feature" of the disorder [1,2]. This physical activity assumes a variety of forms: restless fidgeting, standing and pacing observed on an inpatient unit; exercise routines and walking rituals among outpatients that may consume hours per day. Some activity appears to be goal-directed but may be excessive, such as unnecessary housework, or walking miles per day to get from place to place when other means of transportation exist. Notably, not all patients with AN exhibit increased levels of physical activity, and, in those that do, level of activity may vary over the course of their illness. The range of types of activity, the frequent unawareness on the part of the patient as to how excessive or problematic it may be, and the very driven nature it may assume, make physical activity in AN an intriguing topic for researchers and a critical focus for clinicians working with this population.

Physical Activity: Basic Definitions. The term *physical activity* is used in this chapter to refer broadly to bodily movement produced by skeletal muscles that results in energy expenditure. This includes both *exercise* and *spontaneous physical activity. Exercise* has been defined in various ways including by the intensity of the activity, its context ("structured" or "planned"), its effects (e.g., "with elevated heart rate"), and the underlying goal ("for the sake of fitness" or "recreational" as distinct from "occupational"). The term exercise refers in this chapter to voluntary physical activity of at least moderate intensity that is conducted within a discrete time period and not for occupational purposes. Depending on the purpose of the assessment, alternative definitions may be more appropriate. *Spontaneous physical activity* includes non-exercise motor activity that may or may not be planned, and includes activities of daily living, as well as fidgeting and walking. Spontaneous physical activity is closely related to *Non-Exercise Activity Thermogenesis (NEAT)*, the energy expended for everything that is not sleeping, eating, and sports-like exercise, and varies significantly across individuals [3,4]. For example, it has been suggested that differences in NEAT, as manifested in predilection for more sedentary versus more "active" postures during the course of a day, may contribute to variability across individuals of up to 2000 kcal/day of energy expenditure. More average inter-individual variability estimates are approx 350 kcal/day as for example between lean and obese individuals [5]. Clearly, the role of SPA or NEAT in people with AN requires further investigation.

Definitions: Problems and Pitfalls. As the reader may realize, some patients exhibit behaviors that challenge current categories of physical activity, for example, in the case of a woman who spends 6-8 hours per day doing heavy yard-work, with clear evidence of physical exertion and the intent to burn calories. *It is critical when evaluating patients with AN to take a comprehensive history of their daily physical activity, beyond what they label "exercise."* Inquiry should include means of transportation, and, even if they report use of motorized transportation, determination of how much additional time spent walking to and from the parking spot, subway stop, etc., to their destination. Not uncommonly patients will maximize their time spent ambulating, often without awareness of their behavior. Obtaining a clear and comprehensive history of physical activity by AN patients is helpful to researchers studying exercise behavior, and to clinicians trying to predict an individual's energy expenditure and caloric requirements. Use of a standardized assessment tool such as the International Physical Activity Questionnaire (IPAQ, [6]) may help facilitate recall of physical activity conducted outside of structured exercise.

Exercise: How much is "Excessive"? In addition to the challenge of classifying exercise behavior in patients with AN, both clinicians and researchers face a challenge in determining when it is pathological. At the extreme, e.g., eight hours per day of gym activity, despite injury, the pathology is clear. However more moderate forms of activity, such as one hour per day of moderate-intensity exercise, 5 days per week, is currently the recommendation of the World Health Organization to most adults to maximize health benefits [7]. Because patients with AN by definition have a disorder of energy deficit, any behavior resulting in significant caloric expenditure may be considered unhealthy. Thus, the distinction of pathological exercise in AN is commonly drawn at 5-7 or more hours per week, with or without additional psychological features (e.g., [8,9]).

Excessive Exercise: "Addictive" or "Compulsive"? Qualitative features of exercise are also frequently problematic in AN, with typically very rigid routines surrounding exercise behavior, exercise in the face of injury, compromise of social or occupational commitments in order to exercise, distress or guilt when failing to exercise, and so forth. Several terms have been applied to reflect maladaptive psychological aspects of exercise behavior.

The Addiction Model Patients with AN who engage in high-level exercise often report symptoms listed below [10], which are hallmarks of drug or alcohol addiction. While we prefer to limit the use of the term "addiction" to processes that involve an exogenous agent, it may be helpful to view behaviors, thoughts and feelings associated with exercise in AN patients in light of the types of processes observed in drug or alcohol addictions.

- *Loss of control over behavior*: exercising longer than intended
- *Withdrawal symptoms*: anxiety, irritability, restlessness may occur when exercise is prevented
- *Tolerance*: increasing amounts are required to satisfy the same goal
- *Harmful consequences*: exercise frequently persists despite injury, unintentional weight loss, social or occupational conflicts, or other adverse consequences

Exercise "Dependence" similarly captures the maladaptive role of exercise behavior in an individual's life and includes functional impairment related to excessive exercise behavior, as well as distress when failing to exercise, and "craving" for exercise [11]. Exercise dependence is sometimes separated into "primary" and "secondary" (i.e., to an eating disorder), though it has been questioned whether primary exercise dependence really exists [12].

"Compulsive Exercise" implies that the behavior is driven less by reward than by desire to reduce tension or avoid discomfort. While the term may be suggestive of an anxiety disorder (e.g., OCD), this process is also compatible with the natural course of an addictive process, as people who become dependent to drugs or alcohol commonly report needing to use these substances simply to feel "normal" rather than to experience a "high." The concepts of compulsive exercise and exercise dependence are closely related if not identical.

Scales to quantify the pathological and obligatory aspects of exercise motivation include the Commitment to Exercise Scale [13], the Exercise

Dependence Questionnaire [14], and the Exercise Dependence Scale [15], among others.

Physical Activity in AN: *Why* so compelling? Reasons for exercise in a healthy population are complex and may include desire to be fit, to improve one's appearance, to maintain a healthy body weight or to lose weight; for social interaction; and for improvement of mood [16]. Reasons for exercise in patients with AN are not so dissimilar, though more pathological attitudes towards exercise may be more common, including the experience of intense guilt when exercise is missed, and exercising solely or primarily for reasons of weight, shape or physical attractiveness [17]. A general impression is that *intensity* and *salience* of the drive for exercise are also greater in this patient population. *It is important to keep in mind the complexity of this drive, and that it is rarely* solely *for the purpose of burning calories.*

Restlessness: Patients with AN frequently describe a sense of restlessness and a need to keep moving that sounds not much unlike the phenomenon of akathisia experienced by some patients taking neuroleptic medications. Whether or not this sense of inner tension or restlessness exists as a somatic sensation seems to vary from patient to patient. For patients who do experience restlessness, it may have a physiological basis, presumably related to the underweight state. Candidate molecules include, among others, activation of the HPA axis; reduced leptin levels; and the norepinephrine and/or dopaminergic pathways [18,19]. The existence of an animal model of starvation-induced hyperactivity, or activity-based anorexia, discussed below, underlines the idea that hyperactivity with weight loss is at least in part biologically based. Such animal models should enhance our understanding of mechanisms underlying the drive for activity in AN patients. Identification of such mechanisms may lead to improved pharmacotherapy for restlessness associated with AN.

Affective Regulation: Underweight patients commonly experience dysphoria, depressed mood and anxiety [20], all of which they may attempt to alter by engaging in physical activity. In the general population, exercise is known to have mood-enhancing effects, and may be a useful adjunctive treatment for depression (e.g., [21]). Temporary mood improvement as may occur in AN patients with exercise may be a primary effect of the behavior itself and may also stem from alleviation of eating-disordered cognitions, as mentioned below. Some [8,22,23] studies have found associations between high-level exercise behavior and anxiety symptoms among patients with AN, suggesting that patients may be using exercise as an attempt at *self-medication* for affective or anxiety symptoms. Determination of causality from this association is difficult, however. Alternative possibilities are that certain individuals with AN are more vulnerable to both anxiety symptoms and a proclivity toward exercise; and, that exercise itself *promotes* anxiety in a person with AN. It is conceivable that the cognitive imperative of maintaining a specific exercise routine could generate anxiety, as could, in theory, the biological effects of exercising in a catabolic state [24].

Eating-Disordered Cognitions: Some patients with eating disorders who engage in excessive exercise behavior describe using it to burn calories in a manner akin to purging, e.g., spending four hours running on a treadmill following consumption of an undesired amount of food. Exercise bouts may also occur before an anticipated large meal so that the individual feels safer consuming it. Other patients who adhere to more rigid exercise routines (i.e., not varying by food intake) may also use it as a form of caloric expenditure or modification of weight and shape, even if the stated reason for exercise is otherwise. Such cognitions may be elicited by asking the individual how s/he feels or what s/he thinks will happen when an exercise session is missed.

Habit: The formation of habits and rituals appears to be enhanced in AN for reasons that are not entirely clear, but may inform the compulsive nature of a number of behaviors observed in AN patients, related to eating, checking of weight and shape, and exercise behavior. Exercise in people with AN is typically solitary and often extremely stereotypic, for example, running a set distance each day or performing a specific series of exercises at particular times each day. Such behavior may be related to the underweight state, and/or to trait-based neural mechanisms similar to those seen in people with OCD [25]. Some studies have linked excessive exercise to a higher degree of obsessive-compulsive pathology among AN patients [9,23].

Identity and Social Environment: Patients with AN not uncommonly have a history of performance in sports or dance, and exercise-related activities may hold a prominent role in their sense of themselves as individuals. While some individuals with AN only begin exercising in the course of their disorders, many others have been engaging in high-level activity from a very early age. Often exercise has played an important role in family outings and activities, and family members may be athletic and/or value physical activity as well. Continuing participation in sports events may further reinforce an individual's identity as an athlete.

Health: Exercise is promoted for the general population as a means of protection against cardiovascular disease, cancer, obesity, diabetes, cognitive decline, and osteoporosis, among other illnesses, with fair to strong supporting scientific evidence (e.g., [26]). The average American citizen does not exercise often enough to actualize these health benefits. While patients with AN clearly need not worry about the disorders of overweight, and indeed risk their health by exercising in the underweight state, it is understandable that they may have internalized public health messages in favor of exercise, much in the way they may have internalized recommendations for reduced fat and calorie intake. When addressing patients' thoughts about exercise, it can be helpful to keep in mind that much of the information they have about recommended physical activity is actually appropriate for the average American citizen.

In summary, physical activity in AN is a multifaceted phenomenon that may be reinforced by various processes, both healthy and pathological, and that may be further influenced by the underweight state.

II. Physical Activity in AN: Associated Clinical Problems

Exercise in AN: What's the harm? The message that exercise is detrimental is most often met with extreme resistance by patients with this disorder, for reasons including those discussed above. Patients often experience physical activity as beneficial, and there may be some settings in which exercise may be useful therapeutically to patients with eating disorders, for example, in treatment settings, as a reinforcement for weight gain. Furthermore, physical activity as a mode of transportation and other activities of daily living can be, for outpatients in particular, impossible to avoid. However, as discussed below, several lines of argument and evidence suggest that excessive physical activity, be it exercise or otherwise, may be detrimental to AN patients.

Increased energy expenditure. The degree to which exercise behavior contributes to an energy deficit among people with AN is actually unclear. It is likely that people whose metabolism is suppressed by starvation burn fewer calories for a given degree of exertion compared with normal-weight people. Furthermore the amount of "work" to move a reduced-weight body around during exercise is less than that required to move a normal-weight body. That said, for an underweight person who is trying to normalize metabolism, weight, and eating-related behavior, any energy expenditure above and beyond absolute requirements may be detrimental. Even if frank exercise is avoided, the contribution of lower-level activity such as fidgeting and walking may be significant [3]).

Exercise-related injuries. Injuries due to exercise may be significant, and are likely related to a combination of persistent exercise in the setting of symptoms of strain, and weakened skeletal system, including osteopenia or osteoporosis, in the state of underweight.

Bone density: the good and the bad. In post-menopausal women as well as in healthy young women, exercise is known to have an osteogenic effect [27]. The effect of exercise on bone density in AN is less clearly positive, however. For example, one study that examined associations between regional bone density in both ill and recovered women with AN showed some benefit to high-level bone loading exercise to women exercising while recovered, but a significant detrimental effect to those exercising while ill [28]. Because loss of bone mass is one of the few potentially truly irreversible sequelae of AN, it would seem prudent to minimize any behavior that worsens it.

Amenorrhea. Loss of menstrual cycles is one hallmark feature of AN and is a marker of reduced bone density, likely related to the low-estrogen state underlying each of these phenomena. Among weight-restored women with AN, a significant proportion will remain without menses despite achieving their target body weight. It is likely that persistent excessive exercise behavior acts to suppress resumption of menses in such individuals [29].

Narrowed behavioral repertoire. People who have committed to spending six hours per day exercising logically have six fewer hours per day in which to engage in non-illness-related activities, the very types of activities that would likely facilitate the recovery process. We are not aware of research documenting that choice of exercise over alternative non-eating disordered activities actually contributes to clinical decline. However, this process is all too often apparent clinically when patients describe prioritizing exercise over social, occupational or other activities, as they become progressively underweight and symptomatic.

Reinforcing Eating-Disorder pathology. It is possible, if not likely, that the process of repeatedly engaging in behavior driven by eating-disordered cognitions reinforces the compulsion and the salience of the eating disorder. To the extent that exercise is used as a form of purging, it may also lead to binge-eating among susceptible individuals. Those who exercise daily deprive themselves of the opportunity of realizing that they might actually feel better taking a day off.

Trigger for relapse. Relapse (i.e., weight loss, with or without resumption of problematic eating behaviors) is disturbingly common in AN. At the end of a year following inpatient treatment, some half of patients have lost enough weight to meet criteria for AN again (e.g., [30]). Over long-term follow-up, half or more patients remain chronically or partially ill, while up to 10% have died [31]. Surprisingly little is understood about why AN carries such a high rate of recidivism, or factors that promote relapse in this disorder. However several studies have identified some aspect of problematic exercise behavior or drive as a predictor of relapse in AN [32-34]. Negative findings also have been reported [35], and discrepancies among studies likely reflect varying assessments of exercise or physical activity. That this set of behaviors (i.e., physical activity in AN) may be relevant to relapse, whether as a symptom of an individual already susceptible to relapse or as an underlying proclivity that triggers a patient to relapse after discharge, warrants further investigation.

III. Clinical Management of Physical Activity in AN

The clinical management of the set of behaviors that comprise physical activity depend largely on the degree of illness of the patient and, relatedly, on the setting of care. The below paragraphs describe standard practices currently employed, and areas requiring further research.

Limit Physical Activity. This has been a mainstay approach for inpatient units that treat people with AN. Limitation of physical activity may include: (1) prevention of exercise behavior including by monitoring and limiting or preventing unobserved time; (2) restriction of walking behavior, both on and off the clinical unit; (3) limitation of fidgeting behavior, with staff feedback to patients who demonstrate this; (4) disallowing periods of excessive standing, as this posture itself may be associated with a greater energy expenditure than sitting or lying down [3]; and, ultimately, (5) bedrest, for extremely malnourished individuals. Goals for these restrictions include: (1) reduction of caloric expenditure to shift energy balance in the direction of weight gain; (2) normalization of behavior and prevention of ritualistic behavior surrounding physical activity; (3) prevention of injury, as individuals with AN are susceptible to injury from falling due to a combination of muscular weakness, low bone density, and orthostasis. These limitations are typically maintained by staff observation of patients; therapeutic use of activity monitors may detect additional physical activity that staff may not appreciate and that may escape even patients' awareness. For outpatients, limitations may be aided by discontinuation of gym memberships and clinician monitoring of the patient's reported time spent exercising.

Rethink Exercise. The type of physical activity that typically becomes problematic for AN patients is the solitary exercise or walking that can continue indefinitely, as compared with a discrete exercise class or sporting event. Without a defined endpoint, running, walking or other activities can continue for progressively long periods of time. A statement not uncommonly heard by patients is "I ran [x] miles that day, so I had to run at least that amount the next day." One useful treatment approach, when patients are of a stable enough weight to participate in physical activities, may be to promote goals for exercise that are not calorie-related but focus on socializing, enjoying the process of being active, building strength and improving one's well-being. Yoga, Tai Chi, and other low-impact activities may be therapeutic in this regard. For patients at any stage of treatment who have a history of compulsive, excessive exercise, it may be necessary to disallow the types and opportunities for activities that could facilitate the reemergence of maladaptive exercise behavior.

Address Triggers. Patients with AN often report or exhibit difficulty regulating mood and anxiety symptoms. Such difficulties may lead to attempts to use external means or behaviors to do so – e.g., food restriction, binge-eating, purging, cutting, and drugs, for susceptible individuals. Exercise is one behavior that may be used in attempt to regulate affect in people with AN [36]. Psychotherapy may be helpful in identifying troublesome affective states and providing alternative coping strategies to these problematic behaviors. Addressing and restructuring distorted thoughts that may promote or trigger excessive exercise in particular may also be helpful, as in a CBT-based approach. For example, such thoughts as "I must be active or I'm lazy" or "I will get fat if I don't exercise" could be identified and re-structured with the aid of a therapist.

"Work with it"? Is it possible to harness what appears to be a natural drive in at least some patients with AN to reinforce food intake and weight gain? Indeed, this is an approach that is often employed implicitly on inpatient units, on which activity privileges (off-unit access, participation in gentle exercise) are contingent on achievement of a certain target weight and/or completion of meals. The possibility of explicitly linking individual weights to exercise privileges has been raised [37], as has incorporating more structured therapeutic exercise into treatment of AN [38]. Authors of a recent review of exercise in the treatment of AN concluded that inadequate data currently exist to clearly support an exercise intervention [39], and that further research is warranted.

In summary, the role of exercise during treatment of AN is typically limited, particularly for severely underweight individuals. Physical activity plays an increasing role in treatment and daily life of AN patients as weight restoration progresses. Whether, when, or how frank exercise should be permitted, are questions requiring further research.

IV. Research Topics for Physical Activity in AN

As indicated above, a number of questions about physical activity in AN require further investigation. These fall into the categories of *etiology*, *clinical implications* or *outcome,* and *classification* (i.e., does AN with Excessive Exercise represent a diagnostic subtype of AN?). *Treatment* and how best to tailor it to excessive physical activity warrants further attention. A comprehensive review of research on physical activity in AN is beyond the scope of this chapter. However, one animal model could ultimately prove crucial in the exploration of this behavioral phenomenon in people with AN, and is described below.

Activity-Based Anorexia. One long-known phenomenon that occurs in some rodents subjected to food restriction is that of excessive, maladaptive wheel-running. The model is as follows: rats, which normally eat throughout the dark cycle of the day, are limited to one hour of food intake per day, with simultaneous continuous access to an activity wheel. Animals *without* an activity wheel will lose weight but stabilize their weight by consuming adequate chow during the one-hour access period. Animals *with* activity wheel access will run, in increasing amounts, and eat progressively inadequate amounts of food to maintain their body weight, despite adequate food being available to them in the one-hour period. Rats that develop this syndrome will run up to miles per day on the wheels, with significant loss of body weight, up to the point of death. This striking phenomenon is termed "Activity-Based Anorexia" (ABA) or "Activity Anorexia" [40] and is similar to "Starvation-Induced Hyperactivity" (SIH, or SSIH). That animals in this paradigm starve despite available food, and exhibit paradoxically high levels of physical activity in the face of starvation, has led a number of investigators to discuss its use as an animal model of AN [41].

While ABA is clearly unable to model any of the psychological aspects of AN, "compulsive" running behavior in the setting of starvation does seem apropos of the excessive physical activity seen in a subset of patients with AN. Differences exist in susceptibility to ABA across strains of mice that differ genetically [42], consistent with variability across people in susceptibility to AN, as also likely reflects a genetic basis [43]. The advantage of a rodent model of AN, as with any disease, is that it permits investigation of biological substrates and assessment of possible treatment interventions. It is this author's view that the *strength of ABA as an animal model of AN would be greatly enhanced by limiting its proposed relevance to those patients with AN who are acutely hyperactive*. Improved delineation of excessive physical activity and its correlates in people with AN should prove critical to cross-validation of this animal model.

Findings in ABA Research: A few interesting findings that have stemmed recently from the ABA model are highlighted, in support of its potential utility in translational research: (1) Hyperactivity in ABA is associated with leptin deficiency and reversed with leptin infusions [35,44]; (2) Reduced food intake and weight loss in ABA is mitigated by administration of a corticotrophin-releasing factor (CRF) antagonist [45], suggesting a possible role for corti-costeroids and/or their precursors in maintaining this phenomenon; (3) Weight loss in ABA is mitigated by olanzapine [46], a medication that holds promise for the treatment of patients with AN; (4) Excessive running and weight loss in ABA is mitigated by increasing the ambient temperature [47]. Each of these findings suggests some aspect of pathophysiology and/or treatment of excessive physical activity in AN that may be relevant to the human condition.

Several other findings in ABA, on the other hand, do not appear to map onto the clinical phenomenon. For example, chronic treatment with fluoxetine shows utility in attenuating the phenomenon in rodents when administered prior to the onset of ABA, in at least some investigations [48,49], but little benefit in people with AN after the onset of illness [30]. It is possible that this is because of the timing of drug administration, or other species-specific factors. It is also possible that such discrepancies result from the fact that clinical research typically does not consider exercise behavior when examining biological factors or medication effects, when, in truth, growing research suggests that highly active people with AN have some physiological [50] and/or psychological [9,23] differences from non-exercisers. As stated above, we believe this is an important area for further research.

Conclusion

In summary, physical activity is commonly observed in excess in a significant proportion of people with AN, in a variety of manifestations.

Clinicians are encouraged to take a thorough history of physical activity in this population, including exercise but also non-exercise activity. Researchers have many questions to address about this behavior including its etiology, maintaining mechanisms, prognostic value, and how best to address it in treatment. The field is ripe for such investigations!

Acknowledgment

This work was supported by grants from NARSAD and NIMH (K23071285, R01MH083795).

References

[1] Kron, L., Katz, J. L., Gorzynski, G. & Weiner, H. (1978). Hyperactivity in anorexia nervosa:a fundamental clinical feature. *Compr Psychiatry*, *19*, 433-440.

[2] Casper, R. C. (1998). Behavioral activation and lack of concern, core symptoms of anorexia nervosa? *Int J Eat Disord, 24,* 381-393.

[3] Levine, J. A., Eberhardt, N. L. & Jensen, M. D. (1999). Role of nonexercise activity thermogenesis in resistance to fat gain in humans. *Science, 283*, 212-214.

[4] Levine, J. A., Schleusner, S. J. & Jensen, M. D. (2000). Energy expenditure of nonexercise activity. *Am J Clin Nutr, 72*, 1451-1454.

[5] Levine, J. A., Vander Weg, M. W., Hill, J. O. & Klesges, R. C. (2006). Non-exercise activity thermogenesis: the crouching tiger hidden dragon of societal weight gain. *Arterioscler Thromb Vasc Biol*, *26*, 729-736.

[6] Craig, C., Marshall, A., Sjostrom, M., Bauman, A., Booth, M., Ainsworth, B., et al. (2003). International Physical Activity Questionnaire: 12-Country Reliability and Validity. *Med. Sci. Sports Exerc.*, *35,* 1381-1395.

[7] World Health Organization. Global recommendations on physical activity for health. (2011). *http://www.who.int/dietphysicalactivity/pa/en/index.html.*

[8] Brewerton, T. D., Stellefson, E. J., Hibbs, N., Hodges, E. L. & Cochrane, C. E. (1995). Comparison of eating disorder patients with and without compulsive exercising. *Int J Eat Disord, 17,* 413-416.

[9] Davis, C. & Kaptein, S. (2006). Anorexia nervosa with excessive exercise: a phenotype with close links to obsessive-compulsive disorder. *Psychiatry Res, 142*, 209-217.

[10] Klein, D. A., Bennett, A. S., Schebendach, J., Foltin, R. W., Devlin, M. J. & Walsh, B. T. (2004). Exercise "addiction" in anorexia nervosa: model development and pilot data. *CNS Spectrums, 9*, 531-537.

[11] De Coverley Veale, D. M. W. (1987). Exercise Dependence. *Br J Addiction, 82,* 735-740.

[12] Bamber, D. J., Cockerill, I. M., Rodgers, S. & Carroll, D. Diagnostic criteria for exercise dependence in women. (2003). *Br J Sports Med, 37*, 393-400.

[13] Davis, C., Brewer, H. & Ratusny, D. Behavioral frequency and psychological commitment: necessary concepts in the study of excessive exercising. *J Behav Med, 16,* 611-628.

[14] Ogden, J., Veale, D. & Summers, Z. (1997). The development and validation of the Exercise Dependence Questionnaire. *Addiction Research, 1997,* 343-356.

[15] Symons Downs, D., Hausenblas, H. A. & Nigg, C. R. (2004). Factorial validity and psychometric examination of the Exercise Dependence Sacle -Revised. *Phys Ed Exerc Sci 8*, 183-201.

[16] Bratland-Sanda, S., Sundgot-Borgen, J., Ro, O., Rosenvinge, J. H., Hoffart, A. & Martinsen, E. W. (2010). "I'm not physically active - I only go for walks": physical activity in patients with longstanding eating disorders. *Int J Eat Disord,43*, 88-92.

[17] Mond, J. & Calogero, R. (2009). Excessive exercise in eating disorder patients and in healthy women. *Aust N Z J Psychiatry, 43,* 227-234.

[18] Casper, R. C. (2006). The 'drive for activity' and restlessness in anorexia nervosa: potential pathways. *J Affect Disord, 92,* 99-107.

[19] Adan, R. A., Hillebrand, J. J., Danner, U. N., Cano, S. C., Kas, M. J. & Verhagen, L. A. (2011). Neurobiology driving hyperactivity in activity-based anorexia. *Curr Top Behav Neurosci, 6,* 229-250.

[20] Meehan, K. G., Loeb, K. L., Roberto, C. A. & Attia, E. (2006). Mood change during weight restoration in patients with anorexia nervosa. *Int J Eat Disord, 39,* 587-589.

[21] Hoffman, B. M., Babyak, M. A., Craighead, W. E., Sherwood, A., Doraiswamy, P. M., Coons, M. J., et al. (2011). Exercise and

pharmacotherapy in patients with major depression: one-year follow-up of the SMILE study. *Psychosom Med, 73,* 127-133.

[22] Penas-Lledo, E., Vaz Leal, F. J. & Waller, G. (2002). Excessive exercise in anorexia nervosa and bulimia nervosa: relation to eating characteristics and general psychopathology. *Int J Eat Disord, 31*, 370-375.

[23] Shroff, H., Reba, L., Thornton, L. M., Tozzi, F., Klump, K. L., Berrettini, W. H., et al. (2006). Features associated with excessive exercise in women with eating disorders. *Int J Eat Disord, 39*, 454-461.

[24] Klein, D. A., Mayer, L., Schebendach, J. E. & Walsh, B. T. (2007). Physical activity and cortisol in anorexia nervosa. *Psychoneuroendocrinology, 32,* 539-547.

[25] Steinglass, J. & Walsh, B. T. (2006). Habit learning and anorexia nervosa: a cognitive neuroscience hypothesis. *Int J Eat Disord, 39,* 267-275.

[26] Thompson, P. D., Buchner, D., Pina, I. L., Balady, G. J., Williams, M. A., Marcus, B. H., et al. (2003). Exercise and Physical Activity in the Prevention and Treatment of Atherosclerotic Cardiovascular Disease: A Statement From the Council on Clinical Cardiology (Subcommittee on Exercise, Rehabilitation, and Prevention) and the Council on Nutrition, Physical Activity, and Metabolism (Subcommittee on Physical Activity). *Circulation, 107*, 3109-3116.

[27] Wallace, B. A. & Cumming, R. G. (2000). Systematic review of randomized trials of the effect of exercise on bone mass in pre- and postmenopausal women. *Calcif Tissue Int, 67,* 10-18.

[28] Waugh, E., Woodside, D., Beaton, D., Cote, P. & Hawker, G. A. (2011). Effects of Exercise on Bone Mass in Young Women with Anorexia Nervosa. *Med Sci Sports Exerc, 43,* 755-63.

[29] Jacoangeli, F., Masala, S., Staar Mezzasalma, F., Fiori, R., Martinetti, A., Ficoneri, C., et al. (2006). Amenorrhea after weight recover in anorexia nervosa: role of body composition and endocrine abnormalities. *Eating and Weight Disorders, 11,* e20-e26.

[30] Walsh, B. T., Kaplan, A. S., Attia, E., Olmsted, M., Parides, M., Carter, J. C., et al. (2006). Fluoxetine after weight restoration in anorexia nervosa - A randomized controlled trial. *Journal of the American Medical Association, 295,* 2605-2612.

[31] Steinhausen, H. C. (2002). The outcome of anorexia nervosa in the 20th century. *Am J Psychiatry, 159,* 1284-1293.

[32] Strober, M., Freeman, R. & Morrell, W. (1997). The long term course of severe anorexia nervosa in adolscents: survival analysis of recovery,

relapse, and outcome predictors over 10-15 years in a prospective study. *Int J Eat Dis, 22,* 339-360.

[33] Casper, R. C. & Jabine, L. N. (1996). An eight-year follow-up: Outcome from adolescent compared to adult onset anorexia nervosa. *J Youth Adolescence, 25,* 499-517.

[34] Carter, J. C., Blackmore, E., Sutandar-Pinnock, K. & Woodside, D. B. (2004). Relapse in anorexia nervosa: a survival analysis. *Psychol Med, 34,* 671-679.

[35] van Elburg, A. A., Kas, M. J., Hillebrand, J. J., Eijkemans, R. J. & Van Engeland, H. (2007). The impact of hyperactivity and leptin on recovery from anorexia nervosa. *J Neural Transmission 2007, 114,* 1233-1237.

[36] Bratland-Sanda, S., Sundgot-Borgen, J., Ro, O., Rosenvinge, J. H., Hoffart, A. & Martinsen, E. W. (2010). Physical activity and exercise dependence during inpatient treatment of longstanding eating disorders: an exploratory study of excessive and non-excessive exercisers. *Int J Eat Disord, 43,* 266-273.

[37] Blinder, B. J., Freeman, D. M. & Stunkard, A.J. (1970). Behavior therapy of anorexia nervosa: effectiveness of activity as a reinforcer of weight gain. *Am J Psychiatry, 126,* 1093-1098.

[38] Calogero, R. M. & Pedrotty, K. N. (2004). The practice and process of healthy exercise: an investigation of the treatment of exercise abuse in women with eating disorders. *Eating Disorders, 12,* 273-291.

[39] Zunker, C., Mitchell, J. E. & Wonderlich, S. A. (2011). Exercise interventions for women with anorexia nervosa: A review of the literature. *Int J Eat Dis, 44,* 579-584.

[40] Epling, W. F., & Pierce, W. D. (1991). Activity Anorexia. In: Boulton A, Baker G, Martin-Iverson M, editors. *Neuromethods, Vol 18: Animal Models in Psychiatry I.* New York, NY: Humana Press Inc.; p. 267-311.

[41] Casper, R. C., Sullivan, E. L. & Tecott, L. (2008). Relevance of animal models to human eating disorders and obesity. *Psychopharmacology, 199,* 313-329.

[42] Gelegen, C., Collier, D. A., Campbell, I. C., Oppelaar, H., van den Heuvel, J., Adan, R. A., et al. (2007). Difference in susceptibility to activity-based anorexia in two inbred strains of mice. *European Neuropsychopharmacology, 17,* 199-205.

[43] Thornton, L. M., Mazzoe, S. E. & Bulik, C. M. (2011). The heritability of eating disorders: methods and current findings. *Curr Top Behav Neurosci, 6,* 141-156.

[44] Hillebrand, J. J., Koeners, M. P., de Rijke, C. E., Kas, M. J. & Adan, R. A. (2005). Leptin treatment in activity-based anorexia. *Biol Psychiatry, 58,* 165-171.

[45] Kawaguchi, M., Scott, K. A., Moran, T. H. & Bi, S. (2005). Dorsomedial hypothalamic corticotropin-releasing factor mediation of exercise-induced anorexia. *Am J Physiol Regul Integr Comp Physiol, 288,* R1800-R1805.

[46] Hillebrand, J. J., van Elburg, A. A., Kas, M. J., Van Engeland, H. & Adan, R. A. (2005). Olanzapine reduces physical activity in rats exposed to activity-based anorexia: possible implications for treatment of anorexia nervosa? *Biol Psychiatry, 58,* 651-657.

[47] Cerrato, M., Carrera, O., Vasquez, R., Echevarria, E. & Gutierrez, E. (2010). Heat makes a difference in activity-based anorexia: A translational approach to treatment development in anorexia nervosa. *Int J Eat Dis* [Epub ahead of print].

[48] Altemus, M., Glowa, J. R., Galliven, E., Leong Y. M. & Murphy, D. L. (1996). Effects of Serotonergic Agents on Food-Restriction-Induced Hyperactivity. *Pharmacol., Biochem. and Behav., 53,* 123-131.

[49] Altemus, M., Glowa, J. R. & Murphy, D. L. (1993). Attenuation of food-restriction-induced running by chronic fluoxetine treatment. *Psychopharmacol Bull, 29,* 397-400.

[50] Favaro, A., Caregaro, L., Burlina, A. B. & Santonastaso, P. (2000). Tryptophan levels, excessive exercise, and nutritional status in anorexia nervosa. *Psychosom Med, 62,* 535-538.

In: Anorexia Nervosa
Editor: N. C. Barbarich-Marsteller
ISBN: 978-1-62081-291-4

Chapter 4

PSYCHOSOCIAL TREATMENT OF ADULTS AND ADOLESCENTS WITH ANOREXIA NERVOSA

Zandré Labuschagne, Julianne Faust, Andrea Goldschmidt and Daniel Le Grange*

Department of Psychiatry and Behavioral Neuroscience,
The University of Chicago, Chicago, IL, US

ABSTRACT

Anorexia nervosa (AN) is a serious psychiatric disorder that affects approximately .05% of the population. AN has the highest mortality rate of any psychiatric disorder, and is associated with adverse physical and psychosocial health outcomes. Despite its public health significance, there is a dearth of efficacy data on treatments for AN. Various interventions have been developed, but few have generated successful outcomes in randomized controlled trials. The purpose of this chapter is to systematically review existing evidence-based psychosocial treatments for AN in adolescents and adults. The current literature suggests that family-based treatment is the most efficacious intervention for adolescent

* Corresponding Author's Address: Daniel Le Grange, Ph.D., The University of Chicago, Department of Psychiatry and Behavioral Neuroscience, 5841 S Maryland Ave, MC 3077, Chicago, IL, 60637, Email: legrange@uchicago.edu; Phone: 773-702-9277; Fax: 773 702-9929

AN, as it is associated with significant increases in body weight and psychological functioning across trials. To date, there is no clear treatment of choice for adult AN; thus, identifying efficacious treatments for adults with AN should be a priority. For adolescents, future research should examine alternative interventions for those who fail to respond to family-based treatment.

INTRODUCTION

Anorexia nervosa (AN) is a serious psychiatric disorder that is characterized primarily by a refusal to maintain a minimally adequate body weight for age and height [1]. Other diagnostic features include intense fear of weight gain and disturbances in the way in which body weight and shape are perceived. The Diagnostic and Statistical Manual for Mental Disorders, 4th Edition [1] identifies two types of AN: individuals who do not regularly engage in binge eating or purging behaviors (restricting type), and those who regularly engage in binge eating and purging behaviors (binge/purge type). AN affects approximately .05% of the population [2,3], but despite this relatively low prevalence rate, it entails a major public health concern. AN is associated with significant physical and psychosocial dysfunction, including a high mortality rate, as well as decrements in quality of life [3,4,5,6]. Moreover, AN presents a substantial economic burden, given costs associated with treatment and lost productivity [7,8]. AN has its peak onset during adolescence [4], yet only eight randomized controlled trials (RCTs) have focused on interventions targeting younger populations. The dearth of treatment studies in adults is just as pronounced, with only seven RCTs published to date. Clearly, AN is a disorder warranting clinical and empirical attention.

The purpose of this chapter is to systematically review existing evidence-based psychosocial treatments for AN in adolescents and adults. Treatment approaches that have been employed in these published RCTs (e.g., individual, family, and group psychotherapy) will be reviewed. First, we will provide a brief description of the key characteristics for each treatment modality. Second, a summary of the RCTs that have been conducted for both adolescents and adults will be provided in order to highlight the empirical support for each approach. We will first discuss treatments for adolescents with AN followed by a discussion of treatments for adults with AN.

Literature Search and Retrieval Strategy

Two main databases were utilized (i.e., PsycINFO and PubMed) to search for articles to include in this review. The search terms that we included were: Randomized Controlled Trials, Anorexia Nervosa Treatment, Evidence-Based Treatments, and Psychosocial Treatments for Adults and Adolescents with Anorexia Nervosa, and combinations thereof. We limited our search by type of study, including only outpatient RCTs and evidence-based treatments. In addition, only articles that had been peer-reviewed were included in this chapter.

Treatment Modalities Utilized for Adolescent Anorexia Nervosa

A number of treatment modalities have been utilized for the treatment of adolescents with AN. These interventions often differ in their focus and could include as participants the individual with AN [9,10], parents/ guardians [11], other family members (including siblings and/or extended family members) [12,13], or a combination of these.

A modest number of treatment modalities (individual, family, and group therapy) have been empirically tested in adolescents using RCTs. The following section will only focus on the treatment modalities that have been evaluated in RCTs.

1. Individual Treatment Modalities

Individual Supportive Psychotherapy

Individual supportive psychotherapy (ISP) is not a formal psychoanalytic treatment, but instead is intended to be supportive, educational, and problem-centered. ISP includes elements of cognitive, interpretative, and strategic therapies, and was first employed in the seminal study by Russell and colleagues at the Maudsley Hospital in London [14]. The therapist takes on an active role and helps the patient to understand his or her own cognitions and feelings. Explanations are provided by the therapist regarding the effects of prolonged starvation and its implications for body image, depression, irritability, restlessness, and sleep disturbances [14]. Therapy sessions also focus on aspects of interpersonal functioning in relation to family relationships, school, and social life. Weight is often a factor that parallels the process of therapy: as weight increases, the therapeutic alliance strengthens, while in contrast, if the patient remains at a low body weight, the therapeutic relationship suffers as a consequence [14].

Ego-Oriented Individual Therapy/Adolescent Focused Therapy

In ego-oriented individual therapy (EOIT), the therapist conducts weekly individual therapy sessions with the adolescent while conducting collateral sessions with the parents (without the adolescent) bimonthly. EOIT was first employed in a study by Robin and his colleagues [15], before being re-named Adolescent Focused Therapy (AFT) [16]. During individual sessions, the therapist focuses primarily on the patient's ego-strength, self-efficacy, coping skills, individuation from the nuclear family, and general issues regarding social, physical, and emotional development and how these relate to eating, weight expectations, and body image [15]. In this treatment modality the therapist takes on a nurturant-authoritative stance in that he or she respects the adolescent's autonomy while at the same time being understanding of the patient's effort for autonomy in the midst of his or her struggle with AN. As trust between the patient and therapist increases, the therapist serves as the "tension regulator" by helping the adolescent identify common issues associated with daily life while at the same time offering solutions to promote physical and emotional health. The collateral sessions serve as a means of keeping the parents apprised of the adolescent's recovery, providing psychoeducation about AN, and encouraging parents to be supportive, nonjudgmental, and empathetic [15,16].

Cognitive-Behavior Therapy

Cognitive-behavior therapy (CBT) primarily focuses on cognitions and behaviors that sustain the AN and attempts to make positive changes in areas of self-esteem and interpersonal issues. CBT and parental feedback, as employed by Gowers and his colleagues [17], extends over 12 sessions with a minimum of 4-8 sessions including the parent. Additionally, dietary counseling (DC) and multi-model feedback (weight, self-report and clinician-rated questionnaire) extend over 4 sessions. The purpose of providing feedback to the patient every 6 weeks is to show an association between weight gain and the reduction of self-reported psychopathology [17]. DC is included in the treatment regimen with the aim of establishing a consistent eating pattern while restoring nutritional health.

2. Family Treatment Modalities

Family-Based Treatment

Family-based treatment (FBT), also commonly referred to as the "Maudsley Approach," was first developed in the 1980's at the Maudsley Hospital in London. The primary tenet of this treatment modality is that parents are charged with the task of refeeding the adolescent and reducing symptoms of AN [18,19]. The emphasis is on rapid weight restoration to avoid the immediate and longer-term medical and psychological consequences associated with this disorder. FBT is comprised of three treatment phases. In the first phase, control over the adolescent's eating is temporarily in the parents' domain. The therapist guides the parents and helps them identify strategies for increasing the adolescent's caloric intake and decreasing his or her caloric expenditure in the interest of weight gain. In the second phase of treatment, the patient resumes responsibility over eating, if age/ developmentally appropriate, as the patient is slowly gaining weight and more inclined to eat meals willingly. Finally, in the third phase of treatment, the patient is typically weight-restored and the focus of treatment shifts to address issues related to general adolescent development [18,19].

Two formats of FBT have been investigated, Conjoint and Separated FBT. Conjoint FBT requires that the whole family attend treatment sessions, allowing the therapist to observe family interactions directly [20,21]. Separated FBT is governed by the same principles as FBT, but the patient and the parents are seen separately by the therapist. The parents are provided with a warm and supportive environment and the therapist assists them in taking a firm stance during the process of refeeding their child while at the same time not casting blame on the parents. The patient is seen individually and provided with supportive counseling [20,21].

Behavioral Family Systems Therapy

Behavioral family systems therapy (BFST) combines aspects of behavioral, cognitive, and family systems treatment to help adolescents and their families to overcome AN [15], and is closely based on FBT [22]. The patient, his or her parents, and occasionally siblings are invited to attend therapy sessions. The therapist assists families in implementing a behavioral weight-gain program for their child as he or she is identified as incapable of taking charge of his or her eating habits due to AN [15]. BFST can be divided into three phases of treatment. The first phase of treatment is characterized by asking the parents to take complete control of their child's eating and weight gain. During the second phase of treatment the therapist focuses on cognitive restructuring in addition to nutritional counseling to correct the patient's distorted body image while the patient continues to gain weight. The third phase of treatment starts when the adolescent has reached his or her target weight. With the guidance of the therapist the parents gradually return control of eating back to their child while moving away from the behavioral weight gain program. The adolescent is encouraged to increase his or her autonomy and involvement with peers [15].

Non-Specific Family and Individual Treatment

This particular family therapy modality, primarily employed by Crisp and his colleagues [23], includes both the patient and family members, but to varying degrees. Both the family members and the patient work on issues related to developmental psychopathology but also on issues surrounding weight and food, low-self esteem, ambivalence about patient status/recovery, deficient sense of mastery, and difficulties asking for help [23]. The family takes on an active role in that they are required to establish appropriate boundaries, tackle issues related to conflict avoidance, increase communication about sensitive developmental issues, and develop strategies surrounding problem-solving. These are common issues that arise when the patient starts gaining weight and it is important for the patient and family members to work through these issues and problem solve together as a means of returning to normality within the family environment [23].

3. Outpatient Group Psychotherapy

This treatment modality includes both adolescents and adults and is comprised of group meetings for the patient and separate group meetings for the parents. The groups focus on a series of designated topics, including conflict avoidance, family meaning assigned to weight and shape, communication and relationship skills, sense of self, and identification of moods and their attachments and origins [23]. The same themes are discussed with the parent groups, with the discussion focused on how these issues in their adolescent might affect the family. In addition, the parent groups offer a supportive environment in which families can discuss their shared problems and difficulties. Topics relevant to the eating disorder are discussed while facilitating group problem solving [23].

4. Adjunctive Treatments

Dietary counseling (DC) is typically offered in conjunction with another treatment modality and therefore infrequently offered by itself. The aim of DC is to assist patients in gaining weight at a slow and steady pace [23], and to address distorted thoughts about food, eating, and calories. More importantly, the patient is often given complete autonomy as far as his or her diet is concerned. Meal plans are often suggested as a means of establishing a routine and keeping track of caloric intake. Meal plans are also frequently altered depending on nutritional needs and weight gain/loss.

Randomized Controlled Trials for Adolescents wth Anorexia Nervosa

Few reliable data exist regarding treatment efficacy for adolescents with AN to date. Although AN is considered one of the most serious psychiatric disorders, there has been little guidance in the literature that points to effective treatments interventions for this population [24,25]. To date, only seven RCTs have been conducted for adolescents with AN, suggesting a need for more evidence-based interventions in this population. These RCTs will be reviewed in chronological order.

1. The First Maudsley Hospital Study – FBT vs. ISP Following Hospitalization[1]

Russell and colleagues [14] published the first RCT for AN in which family therapy (FBT) and individual therapy (ISP) for adolescents and adults were compared following a course of inpatient treatment. A total of 80 patients participated. Participants were stratified into 4 subgroups depending on diagnosis [AN or bulimia nervosa (BN)], age of onset of illness, and duration of illness: (i) subgroup 1, patients with AN, age of onset of illness at 18 years or younger, and duration of illness <3 years; (ii) subgroup 2, patients with AN, age of onset of illness at 18 years or younger, duration of illness >3 years; (iii) subgroup 3, patients with AN, age of onset of illness at 19 years or older; and

[1] This RCT included both adolescent and adult populations.

(iv) subgroup 4, patients with BN. All patients had been initially admitted to an inpatient hospital for approximately 10 weeks for weight restoration before being randomized to outpatient treatment. The aim of admission was to restore the patient's nutritional state before embarking on outpatient treatment. The mean weight achieved during inpatient care was 89.5% of average body weight (ABW; expected weight for age and height). Hospitalization prior to initiating outpatient treatment renders this more of a relapse prevention study.

Three categories of general outcome were identified: "good" (maintenance of body weight within 15% of ABW and regular menstrual cycles), "intermediate" (an increase of body weight within 15% ABW, while amenorrhea still persists), and "poor" (less than 15% ABW and the development of bulimic symptoms). Clinical dimensions were measured utilizing the Morgan-Russell Assessment Schedule (MRAS) [26,27].

The main findings for subgroup 1 (i.e., adolescents with a short duration of illness and age of onset before 19 years; *n*=21) showed that FBT outperformed ISP for adolescents with AN at one-year follow-up. Patients in subgroup 1 who received FBT gained significantly more weight (25.5% gain in %ABW) at one-year follow-up when compared to the ISP cohort (15.5% gain in %ABW). Moreover, patients in subgroup 1 who had received FBT gained weight in comparison to their discharge weight (+3.4%) whereas the opposite pattern was seen with patients who had received ISP (-8.3% from discharge weight). Patients in subgroup 1 receiving FBT also showed significantly greater improvements in terms of nutritional status, menstrual function, psychosexual adjustment, and socioeconomic status. The only measure on which the two treatments did not differ was mental status, which the authors attributed to ceiling effects. Findings for patients in subgroup 2 (i.e., adolescents with an age of onset less than or equal to 18 years and a duration of illness >3 years; *n*=15) demonstrated poor outcomes at one-year follow-up irrespective of treatment.

Eisler and his colleagues [28] conducted a 5-year follow-up of all 80 patients, which showed that 90% of patients in subgroup 1 who received FBT continued to do well at 5-year follow-up. These results were based on body weight (maintained within 15% of ABW), regular menstrual cycles, and improved scores on all five subscales of the MRAS. In contrast, approximately 50% of the individuals in subgroup 1 who received ISP still presented with significant eating disorder symptoms five years later.

2. St. George's Hospital Study – Inpatient Treatment vs. Nonspecific Individual and Family Therapy vs. Outpatient Group Psychotherapy[2]

Crisp and his colleagues [23] sought to compare the efficacy of four treatments for 90 adolescents and adults with AN: (i) inpatient care, (ii) nonspecific individual and family psychotherapy in conjunction with DC, (iii) outpatient group psychotherapy (which included the parents and patient participating in the same group) in conjunction with DC, and (iv) a no-treatment control condition. Mean-matched population weight (MMPW) expected weight for age and height, in addition to scores on the MRAS, were used to measure treatment outcome.

All three active treatment groups (i.e., inpatient treatment, nonspecific individual and family psychotherapy, and outpatient group psychotherapy) were successful at helping patients achieve at least 85% of MMPW at the end of treatment. Inpatient treatment participants achieved 100% of target weight and achieved this outcome in a shorter timeframe than the other treatment groups. At one-year follow up, all three treatment groups were able to maintain at least 85% of MMPW, although there were no significant differences between the groups. All three treatment groups showed significant improvements in MRAS at one-year follow-up. Specifically, patients receiving inpatient treatment, and those receiving nonspecific individual and family psychotherapy, significantly improved on the menstruation and nutrition subscales; patients who received nonspecific individual and family psychotherapy also improved in socio-economic adjustment. Patients in outpatient group psychotherapy did marginally well in these domains at one-year follow-up.

Although all three active treatment regimens resulted in similar rates of weight gain, return of menstruation, and improvement in aspects of social and sexual adjustment, the results of this study are difficult to apply clinically. For instance, insufficient descriptions were provided as far as family involvement is concerned. Moreover, adults were included in this RCT and the results were not reported separately for adolescents and adults, making it difficult to interpret how the different treatment approaches work specifically for adolescents. Therefore, the overall findings from this RCT were inconclusive with no clear mandate for one treatment over another.

[2] This treatment study included both adolescents and adults.

3. The Second Maudsley Study – Conjoint FBT vs. Separated FBT

Le Grange and colleagues [21] conducted a pilot study (n=18) comparing Conjoint FBT with Separated FBT for adolescents with AN. Unlike the first Maudsley study [14], patients were treated on an outpatient basis only. Patients and their families completed a battery of assessment measures at three different time points throughout the treatment study (i.e., at the start of treatment, at mid-treatment, and at the end of treatment). Patients provided measures of weight and menstrual status, and completed the Eating Attitudes Test (EAT) [29] and the Rosenberg Self-Esteem Scale (RSES) [30]. Families completed the Standardized Clinical Family Interview (SCFI) [31] and the Family Adaptability and Cohesion Evaluation Scales (FACES-III) [32,33]. Overall outcome was evaluated using the MRAS.

Both interventions produced positive treatment outcomes for patients in terms of weight, eating attitudes, and self-esteem, but neither produced significant changes on measures of family functioning measures at the end of treatment. Conjoint FBT yielded a 13.2% increase in weight while Separated FBT produced a 19.9% increase when compared to the patient's baseline weight. However, the group differences were not statistically significant. Conjoint FBT produced significant improvements on the EAT, RSE, and the total MRAS score for the patient (i.e., the average of the 5 subscale scores), whereas Separated FBT led to significant improvements on the EAT and RSE at the end of treatment.

Although no differences were found on levels of expressed emotion across the two treatment groups, it was noted that families who started treatment with high levels of parental criticism of their ill offspring, remained so throughout treatment. In contrast, families with low levels of parental criticism toward their ill offspring, remained low throughout treatment. While neither treatment appeared to impact family functioning, at least as measured using expressed emotion, both forms of FBT appeared to be effective in reducing AN symptoms in the short term.

Extending The Second Maudsley Study – Conjoint FBT vs. Separated FBT

Eisler [20] extended the Le Grange [21] pilot study by comparing these two formats of FBT in a larger sample of adolescents with AN (n=40). Based on previous findings, which suggest that parental criticism is an important indicator of treatment progress [34,35], treatment assignment for this study was stratified based on the number of critical comments made by the parents towards the patient (two or more critical comments made by either parent was used as the threshold). As was the case for the pilot study, patients and their parents completed assessments including weight, menstrual status, the EAT, the Eating Disorder Inventory (EDI) [36], the Short Mood and Feeling Questionnaire (SMFQ) [37], the RSES, the Maudsley Obsessional and Compulsive Index (MOCI) [38], the FACES-III, and the SCFI.

Assessments were conducted at baseline, 3- and 6-months into treatment, and end of treatment. The end of treatment results show that patients in Separated FBT gained an average of 15% body weight whereas patients in Conjoint FBT only gained 10% body weight when compared to their baseline weight. This difference was not statistically different. Resumption of menses remained at a low rate across the two treatment groups. Only marginal differences were found between the treatment groups on measures of eating disorder symptomatology, but these results consistently favored Separated FBT. The patient group as a whole improved on levels of parental expressed emotion such that critical comments made by the parents decreased while warmth increased (results again favored Separated FBT although no significant differences were found across treatment modalities). Only four subjects dropped out of treatment within the first three months, but there were no differences among the two treatment groups. Both treatment groups produced positive changes in nutritional and psychological measures at the end of treatment, but overall, there were no differences in outcome between the two treatment groups.

4. The First United States Study – BFST vs. EOIT

Robin and colleagues [15] compared BFST to EOIT (also referred to as AFT) in a sample of 58 adolescents with AN. In addition to receiving one of these outpatient treatments, participants met with a pediatrician who determined an appropriate dietary regimen so that the patient would gradually gain one pound per week. Body mass index (BMI; kg/m^2) was utilized to measure nutritional status and considered the primary outcome variable. Since adolescents are still growing, the 50th age- and sex-adjusted BMI percentile was used to measure weight status. Measures of eating-related symptoms [as measured by the EAT, the Body Shape Questionnaire (BSQ) [39], and the Eating Disorder Inventory (EDI) [40]], general psychopathology [as measured by the Beck Depression Inventory (BDI) [41] and the Child Behavior Checklist

(CBCL) [42]], and family functioning [as measured by the Parent Adolescent Relationship Questionnaire (PARQ) [43]] were also administered.

The results of this RCT demonstrated that BFST produced significantly greater changes in BMI percentile when compared to EOIT at end of treatment. BFST achieved a mean change of 5.1% in BMI from baseline compared to 2.7% in BMI for patients in EOIT. At end of treatment, 89% of patients in BFST had resumed their menses compared to 60% in EOIT (results were statistically significant). However, both treatments produced comparable improvements on secondary outcome measures of eating-related and general psychopathology, as well as family functioning. The groups did not differ in terms of dropout rates. Overall, both BFST and EOIT appear to be effective treatments for adolescents with AN, although BFST appears to be marginally more efficient than EOIT in terms of weight gain.

5. The Second United States Study – Short Term FBT vs. Long-Term FBT

As described above, previous studies suggest that FBT appear to be an effective intervention for adolescent AN [14,20,21]. Based on these early findings, Lock and colleagues [44] sought to investigate the optimal length of FBT in adolescents with AN. Two dose conditions, both of which provided standard FBT, were compared. Participants were randomized to either short-term (10 sessions over 6 months) or long-term (20 sessions over 12 months) FBT. Assessments were completed at baseline, and at post-treatment (6- and 12-months for the respective treatments) with the primary outcome measure being BMI. Measures of eating-related psychopathology [as measured by the Eating Disorder Examination (EDE) [45] and the Yale-Brown-Cornell Eating Disorder Scale (YBC-EDS) [46,47], which assesses the severity of obsessionality and compulsiveness related to eating disorder symptoms], general psychopathology [as measured by the Schedule for Affective Disorders and Schizophrenia for School-Age Children (K-SADS) [48] and the CBCL Self-Report Version [49]], and family functioning [as measured by the Family Environmental Scale (FES) [50,51]] were also included.

There were no significant differences between treatment conditions in terms of BMI at post-treatment. However, long-term treatment produced better outcomes on the EDE *eating concerns* subscale, and CBCL internalizing symptoms subscale. Two preliminary moderators of treatment outcome were identified. Patients with high eating disorder related obsessionality, as measured with the YBC-ED, as well as those in single-parent families, did better in long-term FBT rather than short-term-FBT. A total of 9 patients did not complete treatment (defined as attending 80% of treatment sessions), with no significant differences between groups in terms of dropout rates.

Based on these results, most adolescents with AN can be just as effectively treated with short-term FBT as with long-term FBT. Patients with more severe and persistent eating-related obsessive-compulsive thinking at baseline and those with non-intact families appear to respond better to long-term FBT.

6. The Toucan Study – Inpatient vs. Specialist Outpatient Treatment vs. Treatment as Usual

The treatment outcome for child and adolescent AN (TOuCAN) study sought to compare the differences between inpatient treatment, specialist outpatient treatment, and a treatment as usual (TAU) control treatment in 167 patients [17]. TAU incorporated a multidisciplinary approach, which consisted of non-specific family-based treatment, DC, ISP, and medical management. Assessments were carried out at baseline and 1- and 2-year follow-up points, and included measures of treatment outcome as defined by the MRAS[26], emotional and behavioral disorders total severity (clinician-rated) [Health of the Nation Outcome Scale for Children and Adolescents (HoNOCSA) [52] and the self-rated version (HoNOCSA-SR) [53]], eating disorder psychopathology (EDI) [54], family functioning [Family Assessment Device (FAD) [55]], and depression [Mood and Feelings Questionnaire (MFQ) [37]].

At one-year follow-up, all three treatment groups made considerable improvements in terms of weight gain, self-reported psychopathology, and global measures of the MFQ, EDI, FAD, and HoNOCSA. No significant differences were found between the groups, and the mean scores on the MRAS were very similar across the groups. Patients allocated to TAU were less likely to meet criteria for AN at one-year follow-up when compared to the other treatment groups, however, this difference was not statistically significant. "Adherence" (no clear definition of how adherence was measured was given in the article) to inpatient care was poor (49%), which could have compromised the effectiveness of this treatment. Gowers and colleagues [17] sought to compare patients randomized to inpatient treatment to those patients who refused admission and opted to continue outpatient treatment. The results indicate that patients receiving inpatient treatment showed little to no improvement on eating disorder cognitions, such as drive for thinness and body dissatisfaction, when compared to those patients who declined admission.

At two-year follow-up, patients across all three treatment groups continued to improve. Overall, 33% of patients had a good outcome, while 27% still suffered from AN. However, there was no statistically significant difference between the groups. The authors concluded that there is no advantage for inpatient treatment over specialist outpatient treatment or TAU.

7. The Third United States Study – FBT vs. AFT (EOIT)

The most recent published RCT compared FBT with AFT for 121 adolescents with AN treated at two sites: The University of Chicago and Stanford University [56]. The main outcome in this RCT was full remission from AN, where remission was defined categorically as normal weight status (>95% of ABW), as well as a global EDE score within 1 SD of published normative means. Partial remission was defined as >85% of ABW. There were 4 different assessment points (i.e., pretreatment, end of treatment, 6-month follow-up, and 12-month follow-up). Measures included, among others, weight, height, the EDE, and the K-SADS.

There were no significant differences between FBT and AFT at the end of treatment in terms of rates of full remission (FBT=42%; AFT=23%); however, at 6-month follow-up (FBT=40%; AFT=18%) and 12-month follow-up (FBT=49%; AFT=23%) these results were statistically significant with FBT outperforming AFT. Results of partial remission showed greater improvements in FBT when compared to AFT (FBT=89%; AFT=67%) at end of treatment, but these rates did not differ at 6- and 12-month follow-up. Improvements on BMI percentile and EDE scores were greater in FBT than AFT at end of treatment; however, this group difference was not maintained at follow-up. Treatment adherence was good across FBT and AFT with 84% of patients randomized to FBT completing their total therapy sessions, compared to 92% of patients randomized to AFT.

Taken together, the overall findings of these RCTs suggest that FBT is an effective treatment for adolescents with AN, especially for adolescents with a short duration of illness. Moreover, the beneficial effects of FBT are sustained at 4-5 years post-treatment. However, most of the RCTs conducted in adolescents with AN are quite modest in size, which underscores the fact that we should temper our enthusiasm for any one treatment, and also highlights the need for replication with larger sample sizes. Additionally, these findings do not provide clear guidance regarding treatment recommendations for families that are unable to implement FBT or fail to respond to FBT. Finally, more research on moderators and mediators of treatment outcome is needed. We still have scant information about which families stand to benefit from FBT and which families should pursue alternative treatment resources. As a National Institute of Mental Health Workgroup concluded, there clearly is a need for larger, better controlled, systematic research in pediatric populations of AN in order to best guide clinicians in the field [57]. Table I (a) provides a summary of all published RCTs for adolescents with AN.

In the following section, we will first provide a brief description of the key characteristics for each treatment modality employed in RCTs for adults with AN, before providing a synopsis of each of these RCTs.

Treatment Modalities Utilized in Adult Anorexia Nervosa

A modest number of individual therapies [58,59,60,61] as well as family therapy [14,62] have been tested for adults with AN. We will first provide a brief description for each of these treatment modalities, before reviewing the published RCTs for the adult AN population.

1. Individual Treatment Modalities

Behavioral Therapy

Behavioral therapy (BT) applied to AN specifically addresses monitoring eating disorder behaviors, working to eliminate unhealthy habits, and introducing new positive eating behaviors [61]. This treatment typically incorporates use of a diary or record of current eating disorder behaviors. A hierarchy of food-related fears (e.g., specific foods or eating-related situations, such as eating in public) is constructed with the aim of slowly exposing the patient to these fears in a controlled environment. Patients are encouraged to broaden food choices and increase food intake. In addition, relaxation and distraction techniques are introduced during therapy to help patients manage anxiety surrounding eating-related stimuli.

Treasure and colleagues [60] utilized a variation of BT, calling it educational behavioral therapy (EBT). EBT incorporates the principles utilized by BT, with the additional inclusion of educational materials concerning AN, BN, nutrition, and metabolism.

Table 1. Summary of randomized controlled trials for adolescent and adult AN

Study	*N*	*M* Age (Range)	Treatment Conditions	Duration of Treatment	Outcome Measure %IBW*	Treatment Favored
Adolescents + Adults						
Russell et al., 1987	80	21.8 (range=14-35)	FBT vs. ISP	12 months	FBT=90% ISP=18%	Favored FBT for Adoles-cents
Crisp et al., 1991	90	22 (range=16-30)	Inpatient vs. NIT + FT + DC vs. OGP +DC	Several months	NA	No difference
a. Adolescents						
Le Grange et al., 1992	18	15.3 (range=12-17)	CFBT vs. SFBT	12 months	CFBT=70% SFBT=90%	No difference
Robin et al., 1999	37	14.2 (range=12-19)	BFST + DC vs. EOIT +DC	16 months	BFST=65% EOIT=69%	No difference
Eisler et al., 2000	40	15.5 (range=12-19)	CFBT vs. SFBT	12 months	CFT=47% SFT=76%	No difference
Lock et al., 2005	86	15.2 (range=12-18)	FBT (12 mo) vs. FBT (6 mo)	FBT (12 mo) vs. FBT (6 mo)	FBT12mo=95% FBT 6 mo=96%	No difference
Gowers et al., 2007	167	14.11 (range=12-18)	Inpatient vs. SOT (CBT) vs. TAU	6 months	NA	No difference
Lock et al., 2010	121	14.4 (range=12-18)	FBT vs. AFT (EOIT)	12 months	FBT=45% AFT=32%	FBT
b. Adults						
Channon et al., 1989	24	23.8 (range=16-32)	CBT vs. BT vs. TAU	12 months	NA	No difference
Treasure et al., 1995	30	25.0 (range=18-39)	CAT vs. EBT	12 months	CAT=78% EBT=50%	No difference
Dare et al., 2001	84	26.3 (range=19-35)	CAT vs. FDP vs. TAU	12 months	CAT=33% FDP=36% TAU=5%	Favored CAT, FDP over TAU
Pike et al., 2003	33	25.2 (range= 18-45)	CBT vs. DC	12 months	CBT=44% DC=7%	Favored CBT
McIntosh et al., 2005	56	(range=17-40)	CBT vs. IP vs. NSCM	5 months	CBT=31% IPT=10% NSCM=56%	Favored NSCM over CBT, IP

*Good Outcome (Weight >85% IBW or BMI >17.5 at the end of treatment)

Note: FBT=Family-Based Treatment; ISP=Individual Supportive Psychotherapy; NIT=Nonspecific Individual Therapy; FT=Family Therapy; DC=Dietary Counseling; OGP=Outpatient Group Psychotherapy; CFBT= Conjoint Family-

Based Treatment; SFBT=Separated Family-Based Treatment; BFST=Behavioral Family Systems Therapy; EOIT=Ego-Oriented Individual Therapy; SOT (CBT)=Specialist Outpatient Treatment (Cognitive-Behavioral Therapy); TAU=Treatment As Usual; AFT (EOIT)=Adolescent-Focused Treatment; BT= Behavioral Therapy; CAT=Cognitive-Analytic Therapy; EBT=Educational Behavioral Therapy; FDP=Focal Dynamic Psychotherapy; IPT=Interpersonal Psychotherapy; and NSCM=Nonspecific Supportive Clinical Management.

Focal Dynamic Psychotherapy

Focal dynamic psychotherapy (FDP) is a time-limited and focused form of psychotherapy. The therapist takes a non-directive stance during treatment, avoiding making suggestions concerning eating disorder symptomatology and behavior management, and instead focusing on the conscious and unconscious meanings of the eating-related symptoms in terms of the patient's family and history [62,63]. In addition, a particular emphasis is placed on how those symptoms affect current relationships, including therapist/patient transference issues.

Cognitive Analytic Therapy

Cognitive analytic therapy (CAT) for AN combines FDP with cognitive therapy [58,64]. The patient and therapist reconstruct the patient's history and difficulties. A procedural sequencing of events is produced from the history and an interpretation of behavioral patterns surfaces. Cognitive processes are closely examined during therapy sessions. Dysfunctional thought patterns, behavioral patterns, and belief systems are identified and challenged during the treatment process. Interpersonal and transference issues are also addressed during therapy.

Nonspecific Supportive Clinical Management

Nonspecific supportive clinical management (NSCM) also known as Non-Specific Supportive Counseling (NSC), is meant to reflect outpatient care that may be provided in typical clinical settings [58]. The treatment uses education, empathy, and support for the patient in order to develop a therapeutic relationship and encourage adherence to treatment prescriptions [65]. Aspects of supportive psychotherapy are used to praise and encourage the patient with reassurance and feedback. An emphasis is placed on achieving a healthy weight and eliminating eating disorder behaviors. Information is given to the patient concerning these issues as well in the form of verbal instruction and handouts.

Interpersonal Psychotherapy

Interpersonal psychotherapy (IPT), as adapted for eating disorders [66], presumes that AN symptoms develop and are maintained as a means of coping with dysfunctional interpersonal patterns. The first phase of IPT for AN entails taking a history of the patient's life, including important events, the trajectory of eating disturbance, and significant relationships. Major problems are categorized into the domains of grief, interpersonal disputes, role transitions, and interpersonal deficits. The second phase of treatment addresses these identified issues by connecting problems in these domains with onset or worsening of AN symptoms. The last phase of treatment focuses on helping the patient to cope with problems more independently in preparation for termination of treatment.

Cognitive-Behavior Therapy[3]

Cognitive-behavior therapy (CBT) tailored specifically to AN focuses on the behaviors and cognitions that maintain the disorder and works to address the patient's self-esteem, self-concept, and interpersonal issues [67]. CBT takes into account the behavioral (e.g., ritualistic behaviors around meals) and cognitive (e.g., negative body image) components of the disorder in order to implement change in these areas. There are three stages of treatment. The first stage focuses on building the relationship and trust between the therapist and the client, and instigating boundaries for the treatment process. The emphasis during the second phase is placed on changing maladaptive thoughts and behaviors as they relate to food and eating. Behaviors related to food and eating are self-monitored. The final phase of treatment consists of planning for termination and the prevention of relapse once treatment is discontinued.

Dietary Counseling

Dietary counseling (DC) was utilized by Pike and colleagues [59] as a comparison treatment to CBT in a RCT involving adults with AN. Please see this chapter for a summary of this treatment modality.

[3] CBT for adults with AN shares similarities with CBT utilized for adolescents with AN [17].

2. Family Therapy[4]

Family therapy (FT) incorporates family members (including the spouse and/or parents) into the treatment process [62]. An emphasis is placed on helping the patient eliminate eating disorder behaviors as much as possible. FT acknowledges that the illness affects all members of the family, and seeks to remove the eating disorder as a means of controlling the patient's relationships with his or her family members. Most sessions take place with the family as a whole, although occasional individual sessions with just the patient are sometimes permitted. However, during individual sessions, the therapy is still focused on the family dynamics and relationships as they relate to AN.

RANDOMIZED CONTROLLED TRIALS FOR ADULTS WITH ANOREXIA NERVOSA

1. First Maudsley Hospital Study – FBT vs. ISP Following Hospitalization[5]

The first adult RCT to be published was conducted by Russell and colleagues [14]. Study details are previously reviewed in the adolescent section of this chapter, but adult outcomes will be presented here. A cohort of 36 older adolescent and adult patients with AN were randomized to either SFT or IST. These patients were categorized into subgroups 2 (early onset and long duration of AN) and 3 (late onset and short duration of AN) in the study. There were no statistically significant differences in terms of outcome categories (i.e., good, intermediate, and poor, based on %ABW, menstrual status, and presence or absence of bulimic symptoms; see pp. 10-11) between the two treatments at end of treatment for either subgroup 2 or 3. At 5-year follow-up, patients in subgroup 3 overall were found to have maintained benefits received during treatment, with almost 75% of patients rated as having a good or intermediate outcome [28]. There were no differences between patients in SFT and IST in terms of outcome categories at 5-year follow-up. These findings do

---

4 There is considerable overlap between family therapy described in the original Russell[14] RCT and this study by Dare and his colleagues [62].

5 This RCT is discussed in further detail in review of RCTs for adolescents with AN; see pp. 10-11.

not support the benefit of SFT over IST in older adolescents with a long history of AN or adult patients with late-onset AN.

2. Middlesex Hospital, London, Study - CBT vs. BT vs. TAU

Channon and colleagues [61] compared CBT and BT with TAU (consisting of medical monitoring and non-specific counseling by a therapist) in 24 adult patients with AN. The MRAS [26] and the EDI [40] were used to evaluate eating disorder symptoms. In addition, the BDI [41] was used to measure depressive symptoms and the MOCI [38] was used to measure obsessive-compulsive symptoms. Patients were evaluated at pretreatment, post-treatment, and 6- and 12-month follow-up.

Patients receiving TAU had significantly higher scores on the EDI maturity fears scale when compared to CBT and BT at end of the 6-month treatment. Patients receiving CBT, BT, and TAU showed similar improvements from baseline to post-treatment in terms of weight gain, menstrual status, and nutritional function. These improvements were maintained at the 6-month follow-up for patients in all three treatment conditions. Improvements in preferred weight (i.e., the weight that a patient would like to be regardless of medical implications) and the drive for thinness subscale of the EDI were also present for all three groups at 6-month follow-up. At 12-month follow-up, the improvements in weight gain, menstrual status, nutritional function, preferred weight, and the EDI drive for thinness subscale were maintained, with additional improvements on the EDI subscales of maturity fears and interoceptive awareness and on depressed mood evident in all three treatment conditions.

No significant differences were found between the CBT and BT groups overall from pretreatment to end of treatment on any of the outcome measures. At 6-month follow-up, patients in CBT showed more improvement than the BT group in psychosexual functioning and the interpersonal distrust subscale of the EDI, while BT was found to be superior in menstrual status improvement. Patients differed in rates of attrition from treatment, with patients in CBT missing fewer therapy sessions than patients in BT [61]. This study also found that weight gain during treatment was negatively associated with duration of illness, degree of weight loss prior to treatment, age, and laxative abuse.

The results of this study indicate that specialized treatment methods that involve exposure to food-related fears or making changes in a particular belief system may not be any more effective in treating an egosyntonic illness such as AN than TAU. The results also suggest that there is no clear benefit of BT versus CBT in adult patients with AN, but rather that both are equally effective for adults with AN.

3. St. George's Hospital Study – Inpatient Treatment vs. Nonspecific Individual and Family Therapy vs. Outpatient Group Psychotherapy

This treatment study included both adults and adolescents [23]. Results for this RCT did not separate adolescent from adult patients, making it difficult to interpret results for adults. Please see pp. 8-9 for review of this study.

4. Second Maudsley Hospital Study - CAT vs. EBT

Treasure and colleagues [60] conducted a pilot study examining the efficacy of CAT versus EBT in treating a cohort of 30 adults with AN. This study utilized the MRAS [26] to assess eating disorder symptomatology. Data concerning age of onset, percentage of weight loss prior to treatment, duration of amenorrhea, and binge/purge symptoms were also collected. Outcome was measured using categories of good (ABW >85% and regular menstrual cycles) intermediate (ABW >85% and persistent amenorrhea), and poor outcome (ABW <85%). Patients in the EBT group had a mean BMI of 17.4 (BMI at baseline 15.0) by end of treatment, compared to a mean BMI of 18.5 (BMI at baseline 15.6) in the CAT group. These group differences were not statistically significant. Those who were assigned to CAT subjectively rated themselves as more improved than those assigned to the EBT group, although the groups did not significantly differ in treatment outcome using the MRAS. Unlike previous research, this study found that age, BMI, and duration of amenorrhea were not associated with outcome; however, those achieving a good outcome had less severe weight loss prior to treatment than the intermediate and poor outcome groups. There were no differences in dropout rates between CAT and EBT. Finally, patients who dropped out of treatment did not differ from those who completed treatment in terms of any of the measured outcomes.

This study found that outpatient forms of treatment can be effective for older patients with AN with a later onset of illness. An interesting finding of this study included the similarity of outcome in patients who completed treatment and patients who ended treatment early. This may signify that a shorter course of treatment may be appropriate, and even similarly effective, for some adult patients.

5. Third Maudsley Hospital Study - FDP vs. CAT vs. FT

Dare and colleagues [62] evaluated the efficacy of three types of specialized treatments in 84 patients, including FT, CAT, and FDP, as compared to TAU (including low-contact medical management and non-specific counseling)[62]. FDP consisted of weekly sessions over one year [62,63]. FT treatment took place between one and three times per week over one year, as negotiated between the patient and therapist. CAT sessions occurred weekly for the first 20 weeks and then monthly for 3 months. The MRAS [26] was used to assess eating disorder symptomatology.

At the end of treatment, weight gains were minimal across groups, with the mean BMI for all patients changing from 15.4 at baseline to 16.5 at the end of treatment. There were no significant differences between the three specialized treatment groups as measured by the MRAS. There were differences, however, between the three specialized treatments and TAU, with close to half of the patients in TAU gaining no weight at all over the year. When pairwise analyses were conducted, both FDP and FT were superior to TAU in terms of weight gain and reduction of symptoms, although differences between CAT and TAU on these measures did not reach significance. One-third of the patients in the specialized treatments no longer met DSM-IV criteria for AN at the end of treatment, compared to only 5% of patients in TAU. The rates of attrition for all three specialized treatments were comparable, although rates of dropout in the TAU group were significantly higher than in the three specialized treatment groups. Results of this study highlight the benefit of outpatient therapy in treating AN, without the use of hospitalization. It is also of interest to note that patients appear to be more likely to stay in outpatient treatment when offered a specialized treatment versus routine outpatient treatment.

6. First United States Study - CBT vs. DC

A more recent trial compared CBT to DC in 33 patients being discharged from an inpatient hospitalization treatment program [59]. Sessions took place weekly over the year following hospitalization. The EDE [68] and MRAS [26] were used to determine eating disorder diagnoses and symptomatology.

At the end of treatment, a significantly higher percentage of patients in the CBT group met criteria for good outcome relative to the DC group, according to MRAS scales. Furthermore, CBT had a lower combined rate of attrition and relapse than DC. It is also interesting to note that medication effects were found in the CBT group, with 7 of the 8 participants who met criteria for good outcome according to the MRAS scales receiving medication, while only 4 of the 10 who did not meet criteria for good outcome were receiving medication. AN subtype (restricting versus binge eating/purging) was not found to influence treatment outcome overall or by treatment condition. The authors also used a modified definition of recovery that includes meeting criteria for good outcome in addition to the absence of binge eating and purging, and EDE measured eating attitudes and weight concerns within 1 SD of population matched norms. Using this definition of "full recovery" 17% of patients in the CBT group and none of the patients in the DC group met criteria for recovery, although this difference did not reach statistical significance. Patients randomized to CBT remained in therapy for significantly longer periods of time without relapse than those in DC, although the authors did not provide a precise definition of relapse. More specifically, 53% of participants in the DC group met criteria for "relapse" during treatment, whereas 22% of patients in CBT met the criteria.

The research has important implications, as it is the first study to find substantial benefit from any one particular type of psychosocial treatment and also the first study of its kind to use manualized treatment for adult AN [24]. Results suggest that outpatient treatment utilizing CBT is helpful in reducing relapse risk for patients upon discharge from an inpatient hospital setting.

7. New Zealand Study – CBT vs. IP vs. NSCM

The most recent published RCT examining psychosocial treatment in adults with AN (n=56) was conducted by McIntosh and colleagues [58]. This study compared CBT and IPT with NSCM. It was hypothesized that the two specialized treatments would be more effective than NSCM. The EDE [68] and the EDI-2 [54] were used to assess eating disorder symptomatology. The mean BMI at presentation for all patients was 17.3. A symptom rating scale based on the EDE and EDI-2 was used to categorize treatment outcome, with a rating of 1 indicating no significant features of AN present, 2 indicating few eating disorder features present, 3 indicating eating disorder features present but not at a threshold warranting a DSM-IV diagnosis of AN, and a rating of 4 indicating that full criteria for AN are met.

Among all study participants, NSCM was found to be more effective than IPT using the symptom ratings scale. Patients in NSCM had a mean BMI of 18.8 by end of treatment, compared to 18.1 in both the CBT and IPT groups; there were no significant group differences in post-treatment BMI. Using only treatment completers in the analysis yielded a clearer result, with NSCM being superior to both CBT and IPT in terms of symptom ratings at end of treatment. IPT and CBT did not significantly differ from each other in treatment outcome as measured by weight and the EDE scores when analyzing only those who completed treatment. Interestingly, there were no significant differences between the groups in weight and percentage of body fat at end of treatment, both when using all participants and only treatment completers. The results revealed significant differences in baseline weight between those who completed treatment and those who did not, such that treatment completers weighed more at baseline than treatment dropouts. The three treatments did not differ in terms of attrition.

The results did not support the original hypothesis that the specialized treatments would be more effective than NSCM in treating adult patients with AN. IPT was found to be the least effective treatment in this study, potentially because little attention is devoted to overt AN symptoms and there is a possibility of discussing sensitive topics that could trigger AN behaviors. Additionally, despite the differences in outcome, patients perceived all three treatment conditions as equally credible and satisfying.

A long-term follow-up of the McIntosh and colleagues [58] study was done to determine whether there were differences between patients who were treated with CBT, IPT, or NSCM [69]. The average period of time from end of treatment to follow-up was 6.7 years. Over that period of time, approximately 50% of patients across groups were rated as having a good outcome according to the MRAS. Though NSCM was favored at end of treatment over IPT and CBT, those randomized to IPT were most likely to achieve a good outcome rating of 1 or 2 at long-term follow-up, followed by NSCM and CBT; however, group differences were not statistically significant.

The results indicate that although the trajectory of recovery differs between the three treatment groups, they are equally effective at follow-up. CBT and IPT may not be as effective as NSCM earlier on in the treatment process, but produce equivalent benefits over time. The results also suggest that nonspecific supportive clinical management may be sufficient for patients with severe AN. This, in part, could have to do with the flexibility of NSCM, which allows the patient to have some control over the content of the sessions. This type of therapy also stresses the therapeutic relationship, empathy, and support, which may be particularly needed in this population of patients who tend to be socially isolated.

There is no clear treatment of choice for adults with AN as of yet (see Table I (b) for a summary of all published adult RCTs). Moreover, and as noted by Le Grange and Lock [24], patients who have been ill for long periods of time have constituted a large proportion of the samples in the studies to date. Therefore, with no clear treatment mandate in hand coupled with patients who present with a more chronic form of AN, the task of treating these patients is quite challenging for clinicians. With the exception of Pike's quite modest study [59], findings have mostly been inconclusive or even confusing. For instance, Dare and colleagues [62] have found specialized psychosocial treatments to be more effective than routine care, whereas McIntosh and her colleagues [58] have found quite the opposite. Overall, published RCTs for adults with AN have not been sufficiently powered to answer the questions they set out to pursue. Until more sufficiently powered studies can be pursued [70], an effective treatment for this challenging patient population will continue to elude us.

Current Research

While progress in the field of treatment research for adolescents and adults with AN has generally been relatively slow these past two decades, considerable effort is currently being invested in RCTs across the age range. Several studies in the US, United Kingdom and Australia, utilizing FBT for adolescents with AN, are currently underway or nearing completion. While fewer RCTs are underway for adults with AN, several treatment development studies investigating a range of treatment modalities for select subgroups within this patient population are being conducted at this time, or nearing completion. Table 2 provides a summary for these studies that are in progress.

Conclusion

Treatment research on AN has made significant, albeit slow, advances over the past several decades. Evidence suggesting that parental involvement

Table 2. Current Treatment Studies for Anorexia Nervosa

Study	Population	Sites
Adolescents Ages 12-18 years[1]		
Multi-site MGFT vs. FBT	Adolescent AN	University of London (United Kingdom)
FBT vs. SPT	Adolescent subthreshold AN	Mount Sinai School of Medicine (New York)
FBT parent Groups	Adolescent AN	Duke University (North Carolina)
Multi-site FBT vs. SFT	Adolescent AN	Stanford University (California); University of Toronto (Canada); Cornell University (New York); Washington University (Missouri); University of California at San Diego (California); Sheppard Pratt (Maryland); Laureate Psychiatric Clinic (Oklahoma)
Inpatient refeeding vs. outpatient FBT	Adolescent AN	Westmead Children's Hospital Hospital; University of Sydney (Australia)
FBT vs. PFT	Adolescent AN	Royal Children's Hospital, University of Melbourne (Australia); University of Chicago (Illinois)
Adults Ages 18-65 years[2]		
Multi-site CBT vs. NSC	Adult AN	University of Sydney (Australia); University of London (United Kingdom); University of Chicago (Illinois)
Multi-site CBT vs. NSC vs. New Maudsley	Adult AN	University of Western Australia (Perth, Australia); Flinders University (Adelaide, Australia); University of Sydney and Western Sydney (Australia)
FBT-Y	Young adults with AN (ages 18-25 years)	University of Chicago (Illinois)
Internet-based Prevention *IaM*	College-aged women	Technische Universität Dresden (Germany); Stanford University (California)
EABT	Adult AN	University of Pittsburgh (Pennsylvania)
CRT	Adult AN	Stanford University (California)
UCAN	Adult AN	University of North Carolina at Chapel Hill (North Carolina)

Note: MGFT=Multi Group Family Therapy; FBT=Family-Based Treatment; SPT=Supportive Psychotherapy; SFT=Systemic Family Therapy; PFT=Parent Focused Treatment; CBT=Cognitive-Behavior Therapy; NSC=Non-Specific Supportive Counseling; New Maudsley=Individual treatment with family support; FBT-Y=Family-Based Treatment for Young adults; IaM=Image and Mood; EABT=Emotion Acceptance Behavior Therapy; CRT=Cognitive Remediation Therapy; UCAN=Uniting Couples Anorexia Nervosa; [1]All RCTs; [2]Sydney/London/Chicago and Perth/Adelaide/Sydney are RCTs, the remainder are treat-ment development studies.

is crucial in outpatient treatment of adolescents with AN has accumulated [71], and the RCTs that have been published thus far show that FBT is an effective treatment for adolescent AN [56]. The data that are currently available demonstrate that patients do well when there is early weight gain in FBT [72], and that at least two-thirds of patients in FBT reach a healthy weight at the end of treatment, while 80% of patients will continue to do well and remain recovered at 5-year follow-up [28,73,74].However, it remains untested whether FBT's success is due to the active involvement of parents in refeeding or whether similar results can be achieved with a more generic family therapy approach.

Aside from preliminary evidence suggesting that Separated FBT may be more suitable than Conjoint FBT for families with highly critical parents, and that long-term FBT (12 months) may be more beneficial than short-term FBT (6 months) for those patients from single-parent families or with more eating disorder related obsessionality, there is little evidence to guide clinicians in determining who will benefit most from which treatment. The lack of effective outpatient treatment options for adults with AN is alarming given the fact that a longer duration of illness is associated with greater resistance to treatment and more severe long-term medical complications, including high mortality rates [75].

Several future research steps need to be undertaken. Clearly, we should investigate other treatment modalities for adolescent and adult populations. For example, more targeted interpersonal and psychodynamic treatment approaches have not yet been evaluated in the pediatric population. Future research should identify moderators and mediators of treatment outcome to facilitate exploration of matching patients with treatment modality. To date, there is no treatment study that has shown efficacious treatment of adults with AN. It may be useful, as Bulik and colleagues [25] suggests, to consider a stepped-care approach when treating adults with AN, as it is possible that different forms of treatment are more effective at certain points in the recovery process. Perhaps some of the studies that are currently being conducted for adults with AN, and highlighted in Table II, will provide some direction in this regard. Finally, more attention needs to be paid to long-term follow-up care for these patients, since relapse remains all too common [25].

Researchers have made enormous strides in pediatric populations with AN to identify FBT as an effective treatment modality, however we still have a long way to go to determine an efficacious treatment for adult patients with this debilitating disorder.

REFERENCES

[1] American Psychiatric Association. (2000). *Diagnostic and Statistical Manual of Mental Disorders, text revision* (4th ed.). Washington, DC: American Psychiatric Association.

[2] Hoek, H., & Hoeken, D. V. (2003). Review of prevalence and incidence of eating disorders. *International Journal of Eating Disorders*, *34*, 383-396.

[3] Swanson, S. A., Crow, S. J., Le Grange, D., Swendsen, J., & Merikangas, K. R. (2011). Prevalence and correlates of eating disorders in adolescents: Results from the national comorbidity survey replication adolescent supplement. *Archives of General Psychiatry,* (in press).

[4] Hoek, H. W. (2006). Incidence, prevalence, and mortality of anorexia nervosa and other eating disorders. *Current Opinion in Psychiatry*, *19*, 389-394.

[5] Rome, E. S., & Ammerman, S. (2003). Medical complications of eating disorders: an update. *Journal of Adolescent Health*, *33*, 418-426.

[6] Woodside, B., & Staab, R. (2006). Management of Psychiatric Comorbidity in Anorexia Nervosa and Bulimia Nervosa. *CNS Drugs*, *20*, 655-663.

[7] Simon, J., Schmidt, U., & Pilling, S. (2005). The health service use and cost of eating disorders. *Psychological Medicine*, *35*, 1543-1551.

[8] Striegel-Moore, R. H., Leslie, D., Petrill, S. A., Garvin, V., & Rosenheck, R. A. (2000). One-year use and cost of inpatient and outpatient services among female and male patients with an eating disorder: Evidence from a national database of health insurance claims. *International Journal of Eating Disorders, 27*(4), 381-389.

[9] Hall, A., & Crisp, A. H. (1987). Brief psychotherapy in the treatment of anorexia nervosa: Outcome at one year. *British Journal of Psychiatry*, *151*, 185-191.

[10] Garner, D. M. (1986). Review: Individual psychotherapy for anorexia nervosa. In G. I. Szmukler, P. D. Slade, P. Harris, D. Benton, & G. F. M. Russell (Eds.), *Anorexia nervosa and bulimic disorders* (pp.423-434). Oxford: Pergamon Press.

[11] Lewis, H.L. & MacGuire, M.P. (1985). Review of a group for parents of anorexics. *Journal of Psychiatric Research, 19*, 453-458.

[12] Crisp, A. H. (1980). *Anorexia nervosa: Let me be.* London: Academic Press.

[13] Dare, C. (1986). Review: The family therapy of anorexia nervosa. In G. I. Szmukler, P. D. Slade, P. Harris, D. Benton, & G. F. M., Russell (Eds.), *Anorexia nervosa and bulimic disorders* (pp. 435-444). Oxford: Pergamon Press.

[14] Russell, G. F. M., Szmukler, G. I., Dare, C., & Eisler, B. I. (1987). An evaluation of family therapy in anorexia nervosa and bulimia nervosa. *Archives of General Psychiatry*, *44*, 1047-1056.

[15] Robin, A., Siegel, P., Gilroy, M., Dennis, A., Sikand, A. (1999). A controlled comparison of family versus individual therapy for adolescents with anorexia nervosa. *Journal of the American Academy of Child and Adolescent Psychiatry*, *38*, 1482-1489.

[16] Fitzpatrick, K, K., Moye, A., Hoste, R., Lock, J., & Le Grange, D. (2010). Adolescent focused psychotherapy for adolescents with anorexia nervosa. *Journal of Contemporary Psychology*, 40, 31-39.

[17] Gowers, S. G., Clark, A., Roberts, C., Griffiths, A., Edwards, V., Bryan, C., et al. (2007). Clinical effectiveness of treatments for anorexia nervosa in adolescents. *British Journal of Psychiatry*, *191*, 427-435.

[18] Le Grange, D. (1999). Family therapy for adolescent anorexia nervosa. *Journal of Clinical Psychology*, *55*, 727-739.

[19] Lock, J., Le Grange, D., Agras, W. S., Dare, C. (2001). *Treatment manual for anorexia nervosa: A family-based approach*. New York: Guilford Press.

[20] Eisler, I., Dare, C., Hodes, M., Russell, G., Dodge, E., & Le Grange, D. (2000). Family therapy for adolescent anorexia nervosa: the results of a controlled comparison of two family interventions. *Journal of Child Psychology and Psychiatry*, *41*, 727-736.

[21] Le Grange, D., Eisler, I., Dare, C., & Hodes, M. (1992a). Family criticism and self-starvation: A study of expressed emotion. *Journal of Family Therapy*, *14*, 177-192.

[22] Robin, A.L., & Le Grange, D. (2010). Treating adolescents with anorexia nervosa using behavioral family systems therapy. In J.R. Weisz, & A.E. Kazdin (Eds.), *Evidence-based psychotherapies for children and adolescents* (2nd Ed, pp. 345-358). New York: Guilford Press.

[23] Crisp, A. H., Norton, K., Gowers, S., Halek, C., Bowyer, C., Yeldam, D., Bhat, A. (1991). A controlled study of the effect of therapies aimed at adolescent and family psychopathology in anorexia nervosa. *Journal of Psychiatry, 159*, 325-333.

[24] Le Grange, D., & Lock, J. (2005). The dearth of psychological treatment studies for anorexia nervosa. *International Journal of Eating Disorders, 37*, 79-81.

[25] Bulik, C. M., Berkman, N. D., Brownley, K.A., Sedway, J. A., & Lohr, K. N. (2007). Anorexia Nervosa treatment: a systematic review of randomized controlled treatment trials. *International Journal of Eating Disorders*, *40*, 310-320.

[26] Morgan, H. G., Hayward, A. E. (1988). Clinical Assessment of anorexia nervosa: the Morgan-Russell outcome assessment schedule. *British Journal of Psychiatry*, *152*, 367-371.

[27] Morgan, H. G., & Russell, G. F. M. (1975). Value of family background and clinical features as predictors of long-term outcome in anorexia nervosa: Four-year follow-up study of 41 patients. *Psychological Medicine*, *5*, 355-371.

[28] Eisler, I., Dare, C., Russel, G. F. M., Szmukler, G. I., Le Grange, D., & Dodge, E. (1997). Family and individual therapy in anorexia nervosa: A five-year follow-up. *Archives of General Psychiatry*, *54,* 1025-1030.

[29] Garner, D. M., & Garfinkel, P. E. (1979). The Eating Attitude Test: An index of the symptoms of anorexia nervosa. *Psychological Medicine*, *9*, 273-279.

[30] Rosenberg, M. (1965). *Society and the adolescent self-image*. Princeton, NJ: University Press.

[31] Kinston, W., & Loader, P. (1984). Eliciting whole-family interaction with the standardized clinical interview. *Journal of Family Therapy*, *6,* 347-363.

[32] Olson, D. H., Sprenkle, D. H., & Russell, C. S. (1979). Circumplex Model of marital and family systems: I. Cohesion and Adaptability dimensions, family types and clinical applications. *Family Process*, *18*, 3-28.

[33] Olson, D. H., Portner, J., & Lavee, Y. (1985). *FACES III*. St. Paul, MN: Family Social Science, University of Minnesota.

[34] Le Grange, D., Eisler, I., Dare, C., & Russell, G. F. M. (1992b). Evaluation of family therapy in anorexia nervosa: A pilot study. *International Journal of Eating Disorders,12*, 347-357.

[35] Szmukler, G. I., Eisler, I, Russell, G. F. M., & Dare, C. (1985). Parental "Expressed Emotion", anorexia nervosa and dropping out of treatment. *British Journal of Psychiatry*, *147,* 265-271.

[36] Garner, D. M., Olmstead, M. P., & Polivy, J. (1983). Development and validation of multidimensional eating disorder inventory for anorexia nervosa and bulimia. *International Journal of Eating Disorder*, 2, 15-34.

[37] Angold, A., Costello, E. J., Messer, S. C., & Pickels, A. (1995). Development of short questionnaire for use in epidemiological studies of depression in children and adolescents. *International Journal of Methods in Psychiatric Research*, *5*, 237-249.

[38] Hodgson, R. J., & Rachman, S. (1977). Obsessional-compulsive complaints. *Behavior Research and Therapy*, 15, 389-395.

[39] Cooper, P. J., Taylor, M. J., Cooper, Z., Fairburn, C.G. (1987). The development and validation of the Body Shape Questionnaire. *International Journal of Eating Disorders*, *6*, 485-494.

[40] Garner, D. M., Olmstead, M. P. (1984). *Manual for the Eating Disorder Inventory*. Odessa, FL: Psychological Assessment Resources.

[41] Beck, A. (1967). *Depression: Clinical, Experimental, and Theoretical Aspects*. New York: Hoeber.

[42] Achenbach, T. M., & Edelbrock, C. (1983). *Manual for the Child-Behavior Checklist*. Burlington: University of Vermont, Department of Psychiatry.

[43] Robin, A. L., Koepke, T., & Moye, A. (1990). Multidimensional assessment of parent-adolescent relations. *Psychological Assessment and Journal Consultant of Clinical Psychologists*, *2*, 451-459.

[44] Lock, J., Agras, W. S., Bryson, S., & Kraemer, H. (2005). A comparison of short- and long-term family therapy for adolescent anorexia nervosa. *Journal of the American Academy of Child and Adolescent Psychiatry*, *44*, 632-639.

[45] Cooper, Z., Cooper, P. J, & Fairburn, C. G. (1989). The validity of the eating disorder examination and its subscales. *British Journal of Psychiatry*. *154*, 807-812.

[46] Mazure, S., Halmi, S., Sunday, S., Romano, S., & Einhorn, A. (1994). The Yale-Brown-Cornell Eating Disorder Scale: development, use, reliability, and validity. *Journal of Psychiatric Research*, *28*, 425-445.

[47] [47] Mazure, S., Halmi, C., & Einhorn, A. (1995). The Yale-Brown-Cornell Eating Disorder Scale: a new scale to assess eating disorder symptomatology. *International Journal of Eating Disorders*, *18*, 237-245.

[48] Kaufman, J., Birmhaher, B., Brent, D., Rao, U., Flynn, C., Morici, P., Ryan, M. (1997). Schedule for affective disorders and schizophrenia for school-age children-present and lifetime version (KSADS-PL): initial

reliability and validity data. *Journal of the American Child and Adolescent Psychiatry*. *36*, 980-988.

[49] Achenbach, T. (1991). *Manual for the Child-Behavior Checklist 14-18 and 1991 Profile.* Burlington: University of Vermont, Department of Psychiatry.

[50] Moos, R. (1974). *The family environmental scale, Form R.* Palo Alto, CA: Consulting Psychologists Press.

[51] Moos, R., & Moos, B. (1994). *The Family Environment Scale Manual.* Palo Alto, CA: Consulting Psychologists Press.

[52] Gowers, S. G., Harrington, R, C., Whitton, A., et al. (1999). Brief scale for measuring the outcomes of emotional and behavioral disorders in children, Health of the Nation Outcome Scales for Children and Adolescents (HoNOCSA). *British Journal of Psychiatry*, *174*, 413-416.

[53] Gowers, S. G., Levine, W., Bailey-Rogers, S., Shore, A., & Burhouse, E. (2002). The use of a routine self-report outcome measure (HoNOCSA-SR) in two adolescent mental health services. *British Journal of Psychiatry*, *180*, 266-269.

[54] Garner, D.M. (1991). *Eating Disorder Inventory-2.* Odessa, FL: Psychological Assessment Resources.

[55] Epstein, N., Bishop, D, & Levin, S. (1983). The McMaster Family Assessment Device. *Journal of Marital and Family Therapy*, *9*, 170-180.

[56] Lock, J., Le Grange, D., Agras, W. S., Moye, A., Bryson, S., & Booil, J. (2010). Randomized Clinical Trial Comparing Family-Based Treatment with Adolescent-Focused Individual Therapy for Adolescents with Anorexia Nervosa. *Archives of General Psychiatry*, *67*(10), 1025-1032.

[57] Agras, W, S., Brandt, H., Bulik, C. M., Dolan-Sewell, R., Fairburn, C. G., Halmi, C. A., Wilfley, D.E. (2004). Report of the National Health Institutes of Health Workshop on Overcoming barriers to treatment research in anorexia nervosa. *International Journal of Eating Disorders*, *35,* 509-521.

[58] McIntosh, V. V. W., Jordan, J., Carter, F. A., Luty, S. E., McKenzie, J. M., Bulik, C. M., & Joyce, P. R. (2005). Three psychotherapies for anorexia nervosa: A randomized, controlled trial. *The American Journal of Psychiatry, 162*, 741-747.

[59] Pike, K. M., Walsh, B. T., Vitousek, K., Wilson, G. T., & Bauer, J. (2003). Cognitive behavior therapy in the posthospitalization treatment of anorexia nervosa. *The American Journal of Psychiatry, 160*, 2046-2049.

[60] Treasure, J., Todd, G., Brolly, M., Tiller, J., Nehmed, A., & Denman, F. (1995). A pilot study of randomized trial of cognitive analytical therapy vs. educational behavioral therapy for adult anorexia nervosa. *Behavior Research and Therapy, 33*, 363-367.

[61] Channon, S., De Silva, P., Hemsley, D., & Perkins, R. E. (1989). A controlled trial of cognitive-behavioral and behavioral treatment of anorexia nervosa. *Behavior Research and Therapy, 27*, 529-535.

[62] Dare, C., Eisler, I., Russell, G., Treasure, J., & Dodge, L. (2001). Psychological therapies for adults with anorexia nervosa: Randomized controlled trial of outpatient treatments. *British Journal of Psychiatry, 178*, 216-221.

[63] Malan, D. H. (1976). *Toward the validation of dynamic psychotherapy: A replication*. Oxford, England: Plenum.

[64] Ryle, A. (1990). *Cognitive-analytic therapy: Active participation in change*. Chichester: Wiley.

[65] Joyce, P. R. (1995). The clinical management of depression. In P. R. Joyce., S. E. Romans., P. M. Ellis., & T. S. Silverstone (Eds.). *Affective Disorders* (pp. 35-45). Christchurch, NZ: Department of Psychological Medicine.

[66] Fairburn, C.G. (1993). Interpersonal psychotherapy for bulimia nervosa. In G.L. Klerman & M.M. Weissman MM (Eds.). New Applications of Interpersonal Psychotherapy (pp. 355-378). Washington, DC: American Psychiatric Press.

[67] Garner, D. M., Vitousek, K. M., & Pike, K. M. (1997). Cognitive-behavioral therapy for anorexia nervosa. In D. M., Garner & P. E., Garfinkel (Eds.). *Handbook for Treatment of Eating Disorders* (pp. 94-144). New York: Guilford Press.

[68] Fairburn, C. G., & Cooper, Z. (1993). The eating disorder examination (12th ed.). In C. G. Fairburn & G. T. Wilson (Eds.) *Binge eating: Nature, assessment and treatment* (pp. 317-360). New York: Guilford Press.

[69] Carter, F. A., Jordan, J., McIntosh, V. V. W., Luty, S. E., McKenzie, J. M., Frampton, C. M. A., & Joyce, P. R. (2010). The long-term efficacy of three psychotherapies for anorexia nervosa: A randomized, controlled trial. *International Journal of Eating Disorders,* (in press).

[70] Halmi, K.A., Agras, W.S., Crow, S., Mitchell, J., Wilson, G.T., Bryson, S.W., Kraemer, H.C. (2005). Predictors of treatment acceptance and completion in anorexia nervosa: implications for future study design. *Archives of General Psychiatry*, 62, 776-781.

[71] Le Grange, D., & Eisler, I. (2009). Family interventions in adolescent anorexia nervosa. *Child and Adolescent Psychiatric Clinics of North America*, *18*, 159-173.

[72] Doyle, P., Le Grange, D., Celio-Doyle, A., Loeb, K., & Crosby, R. (2010). Early response to family-based treatment for adolescent anorexia nervosa. *International Journal of Eating Disorders*, 43, 659-662.

[73] Eisler, I., Simic, M., Russell, G. F. M., & Dare, C. (2007). A randomized controlled treatment trial of two forms of family therapy in adolescent anorexia nervosa: A five-year follow-up. *Journal of Child Psychology and Psychiatry*, *48,* 552-560.

[74] Lock, J., Couturier, J., & Agras, W. S. (2006). Comparison of long-term outcomes in adolescents treated with family therapy. *Journal of the American Academy of Child and Adolescent Psychiatry*, *45*, 666-672.

[75] Powers, P. S., & Bannon, Y. (2004). Medical comorbidity of anorexia nervosa, bulimia nervosa, and binge eating disorder. In T. D. Brewerton (Ed.), *Clinical handbook of eating disorders: An integrated approach* (pp. 231-255). New York: Marcel Dekker.

In: Anorexia Nervosa
Editor: N. C. Barbarich-Marsteller
ISBN: 978-1-62081-291-4

Chapter 5

PHARMACOLOGICAL TREATMENTS FOR ANOREXIA NERVOSA

***Nicole C. Barbarich-Marsteller*[*a,b], *Kevin Laurino*[a] *and Anna Rita Colacino*[a]**
[a]Department of Psychiatry, College of Physicians and Surgeons of Columbia University, New York, NY, US
[b]New York State Psychiatric Institute, New York, NY, US

ABSTRACT

Despite the high rates of comorbidity with depression and anxiety disorders, as well as the significant neurotransmitter alterations present during starvation, pharmacological treatments targeting the serotonin and dopamine system have had surprisingly little efficacy in the treatment of anorexia nervosa. As this chapter reviews, there is no clear evidence to support the use of typical antipsychotics or antidepressants in the treatment of anorexia nervosa. While atypical antipsychotics provide the most promising line of pharmacological treatment when used as an adjunct to other treatments, these drugs are only effective for some individuals with anorexia nervosa. Additional research is clearly needed to identify the biological systems that perpetuate the unrelenting self-starvation in individuals with anorexia nervosa, in order to develop

---

* Please send correspondence to: Nicole C. Barbarich-Marsteller, Ph.D., Columbia University, NYSPI, 1051 Riverside Drive, Unit 98, New York, NY 10032, Phone: (212) 543-5197, Fax: (212) 543-5607, nbarbarich@yahoo.com

targeted pharmacological treatments aimed at modulating the maladaptive behaviors characteristic of this deadly disease.

Keywords: anorexia nervosa, eating disorders, starvation, pharmacological treatments, drug treatments

INTRODUCTION

The course of anorexia nervosa is often variable, with some individuals recovering after the initial episode while others follow a more chronic course characterized by partial weight restoration, repeated relapses, crossover to bulimia nervosa, and high rates of mortality [1-7]. Treatment strategies are limited (see Chapter 4 for a review of psychosocial treatments and [8]) and pharmacological treatments in particular have had limited efficacy during the acute phase of illness, in improving psychiatric comorbidity, or in preventing relapse [9, 10]. It is unclear why pharmacological treatments have been ineffective in individuals with anorexia nervosa [11], particularly given the high rates of comorbidity with depression and anxiety disorders (for example, [12, 13]) and the usefulness of pharmacological treatments in mediating symptoms in these disorders.

A major hurdle in developing successful pharmacological treatments for anorexia nervosa has been a lack of an understanding of the neurobiological mechanisms that drive the unrelenting self-starvation and, commonly, the hyperactivity exhibited by affected individuals. Factors that initiate the onset of dieting may be distinct from factors that maintain self-starvation once weight loss occurs [14]. Factors maintaining self-starvation likely include psychological as well as physiological processes, and while a number of biological abnormalities have been identified in underweight individuals with anorexia nervosa, the degree to which they are causal remains unclear [14]. For example, a wide range of biological abnormalities have been described in anorexia nervosa but treatments aimed at correcting these abnormalities generally do not lead to significant improvement. It is not clear whether the lack of efficacy of pharmacological treatments for anorexia nervosa is due to partial or ineffective drug metabolism related to severe starvation, or whether the drugs administered are targeting systems that are not primarily involved in the development and/or maintenance of anorexia nervosa.

Table 1. Summary of findings from pharmacological treatment studies in anorexia nervosa

Study	Drug	Control	Study Design	Age of subjects	N	Outcome
Typical Antipsychotics (TA)						
[15]	Chlorpromazine + Insulin	bed rest and high calorie diets	open trial case histories	adolescents adults	57	combined treatment resulted in more rapid weight gain in hospitalized patients, but had no significant effect on long-term outcome
[16]	Pimozide	behavior therapy	open trial	adolescents	10	pimozide did not augment weight gain associated with behavior therapy
[17]	Pimozide	placebo	double-blind placebo-controlled cross-over analysis	adolescents adults	18	pimozide was associated with some improvement in attitude towards treatment and a trend towards weight gain when added to behavior therapy
[18]	Sulpiride	placebo	double-blind placebo-controlled cross-over analysis	adolescents adults	18	sulpiride was associated with an early effect on weight gain, but cross-over analysis did not reach statistical significance
[19]	Haloperidol	none	open trial	adults	13	haloperidol was associated with some improvement in BMI and symptoms when added to standard treatment
Tricyclic Antidepressants (TCA)						
[20]	Clomipramine	placebo	randomized double-blind placebo-controlled	adults	16	clomipramine was associated with increased hunger, appetite, energy intake, more stable eating habits and body weight maintenance, but also a reduced rate of weight gain during inpatient treatment
[21]	Clomipramine	placebo	randomized double-blind	adolescents adults	16	clomipramine was associated with increased appetite, hunger and calorie consumption during the early stages of inpatient treatment, but no impact on outcome
[22]	Amitriptyline	placebo or psychosocial treatment only	double-blind placebo-controlled	adolescents adults	43	amitriptyline had no significant effect on outcome
Selective Serotonin Reuptake Inhibitors (SSRI)						

Table 1. (Continued)

Study	Drug	Control	Study Design	Age of subjects	N	Outcome
[26]	Fluoxetine	none	case report	adult	1	fluoxetine was associated with improvements in weight, mood, and eating disorder symptomatology in an individual with a chronic course
[27]	Fluoxetine	none	open trial	adults	6	fluoxetine was associated with improvement in depressive symptoms which was associated with weight gain
[28]	Fluoxetine	matched historical case-controls without fluoxetine	open trial	adolescents adults	66	fluoxetine had no therapeutic benefit when added to inpatient therapy
[29]	Fluoxetine	placebo	randomized double-blind placebo-controlled	adolescents adults	31	fluoxetine had no therapeutic benefit when added to inpatient treatment
[30]	Nutritional Management + Fluoxetine	nutritional management alone	single blind	adults	95	fluoxetine was associated with a more rapid and greater increase in BMI and a decrease in physical exercise
[31]	Fluoxetine + Nutritional Supplements	fluoxetine + nutritional placebo	double-blind placebo-controlled	adults	26	nutritional supplements were not effective in increasing the efficacy of fluoxetine in underweight individuals with anorexia nervosa
[32]	Fluoxetine	none	open trial	adults	31	fluoxetine was associated with some efficacy in maintaining weight after inpatient discharge
[33]	Fluoxetine	matched historical case-controls without fluoxetine	prospective longitudinal follow-up	adolescents adults	66	adjunctive fluoxetine treatment had no additive long-term therapeutic benefit when measured against the effects of sustained and intensive follow-up treatment
[34]	Fluoxetine	placebo	double-blind placebo-controlled	adolescents adults	35	fluoxetine was associated with reduced relapse as determined by a significant increase in weight and a reduction in symptoms
[35]	Fluoxetine	placebo	randomized double-blind placebo-controlled	adolescents adults	93	fluoxetine had no significant effect on relapse when added to outpatient treatment following intensive inpatient treatment

Study	Drug	Control	Study Design	Age of subjects	N	Outcome
[36]	Citalopram	none	open trial	adolescents adults	32	citalopram was associated with a satisfactory response to treatment with some improvement in weight and symptomatology in approximately half of patients
[37]	Citalopram	none	open trial	adults	6	citalopram was associated with decreased body dissatisfaction when added to systemic psychotherapy
[38]	Citalopram	wait-listed	randomized	adolescents adults	52	citalopram was associated with some improvement in depression, obsessive-compulsive symptoms, impulsiveness, and trait-anger, but no difference in weight gain during outpatient treatment
[39]	Fluoxetine, Fluvoxamine, or Sertraline	no SSRI	retrospective case analysis	children adolescents	32	SSRI treatment had no therapeutic benefit when added to inpatient and outpatient treatment
[40]	Fluoxetine or Venlafaxine	none	randomized	adults	24	venlafaxine and fluoxetine were associated with an increased BMI and reduced psychopathology when combined with cognitive behavioral therapy in atypical AN; venlafaxine was also associated with reduced anxiety
[42]	Sertraline	none	case reports	adolescents	5	sertraline was associated with weight restoration and a decrease in core eating disorder symptoms, depression, and obsessional thoughts when added to other treatments
[43]	Sertraline	no medication	open trial	adolescents adults	22	sertraline was not associated with weight restoration, but was associated with a greater reduction in depressive symptoms, perfectionist attitudes, ineffectiveness, and lack of interoceptive awareness
Tetracyclic antidepressants (TeCA)						
[45]	Mirtazapine	none	case report	adult	1	mirtazapine was associated with weight gain and improvements in depression

Table 1. (Continued)

Study	Drug	Control	Study Design	Age of subjects	N	Outcome
[46]	Mirtazapine	no drug	case control	adolescent	18	mirtazapine had no significant effect on weight or BMI
Atypical Antipsychotics (AA)						
[47]	Olanzapine	none	case reports	adult	3	olanzapine was associated with improvements in body weight, appetite and body image
[48]	Olanzapine	none	case reports	adolescents adults	2	olanzapine was associated with weight gain and maintenance and reduced agitation and resistance to treatment
[49]	Olanzapine	none	case report	adolescents children	5	olanzapine was associated with improvements in severe psychopathology which ultimately allowed for better cooperation between patient and therapist in increasing weight gain
[50]	Olanzapine	none	open trial	adolescents adults	18	olanzapine was associated with some weight gain in an outpatient setting
[51]	Olanzapine	none	retrospective case reports	adults	14	olanzapine alone and in conjunction with other psychotropic treatments was associated with an improvement in BMI during inpatient hospitalization
[53]	Olanzapine	none	case reports	children	4	olanzapine was associated with weight gain and maintenance, a decrease in levels of agitation and premeal anxiety, and improvements in sleep, general functioning, and overall compliance with inpatient treatment
[54]	Olanzapine	none	open trial	adolescents adults	18	in a retrospective interview regarding drug response, olanzapine was associated with reductions in anxiety, difficulty eating, and core eating disorder symptoms
[55]	Olanzapine	Com-pared to histo-rical case controls	open trial	adolescents adults	17	olanzapine was associated with a reduction in depression, anxiety, and core eating disorder symptoms and an increase in weight

Study	Drug	Control	Study Design	Age of subjects	N	Outcome
[56]	Olanzapine	no medication	open trial	adolescents adults	18	olanzapine was associated with reduced activity levels, but no effect on body weight during inpatient or outpatient treatment
[57]	Olanzapine	none	case reports	adolescents	5	olanzapine was associated with an increase in BMI when combined with psychotherapy; a dose above 5 mg was associated with decreased anxiety and rumination and improved sleep
[58]	Olanzapine	none	open trial	children adolescents	13	olanzapine was associated with significant improvements in weight, global functioning, eating attitudes, anxious-depressive symptoms and hyperactivity
[59]	Olanzapine	placebo	Random-ized double-blind placebo-controlled	adults	30	olanzapine was associated with improvements in numerous aspects of treatment when combined with cognitive behavioral therapy, with some differences between anorexia nervosa subtypes
[60]	Olanzapine	placebo	randomized double-blind placebo-controlled	adolescents	34	olanzapine was associated with a greater rate of increase in weight, earlier achievement of target body mass index, and a greater rate of decrease in obsessive symptoms when combined with hospital day treatment
[61]	Olanzapine	placebo	double-blind placebo-controlled	adults	20	olanzapine did not augment weight gain induced by cognitive-behavioral psychotherapy and programmed nutritional rehabilitation
[62]	Olanzapine	placebo	double-blind placebo-controlled	children adolescents adults	20	olanzapine did not augment treatment when added to a comprehensive eating disorders treatment program
[73]	Olanzapine	placebo	Random-ized double-blind placebo-controlled	adolescents	--	results not currently available
[74]	Olanzapine	no medication	matched group com-parison	adolescents	86	unable to draw any firm conclusions regarding the efficacy of olanzapine

Table 1. (Continued)

Study	Drug	Control	Study Design	Age of subjects	N	Outcome
[64]	Risperidone	none	case study	adolescent	1	risperidone was associated with a decrease in agitation and aggression, loss of paranoid ideation, and improvements in behavior in a patient with comorbid autism disorder
[65]	Risperidone	none	case reports	adolescents	2	risperidone was associated with an increase in BMI along with improvements in body image disturbance and food perception
[66]	Risperidone	placebo	double-blind placebo-controlled	children adolescents adults	40	risperidone had no therapeutic benefit during the weight restoration phase of care when added to an eating disorders treatment program
[67]	Quetiapine	none	open label	adult	8	quetiapine was associated with a significant improvement in restrictive eating when added to a specialist multidisciplinary treatment
[68]	Quetiapine	none	open trial	children adolescents adults	19	quetiapine was associated with a reduction in depression, anxiety, and obsessive compulsive symptoms
[69]	Quetiapine	none	case reports	children adolescents	3	quetiapine was associated with improvements in psychopathology
[70]	Quetiapine	treatment as usual	naturalistic open label randomized controlled trial	adolescents adults	33	quetiapine was associated with a trend towards both psychological and physical improvements
[72]	Aripiprazole	none	case reports	adults	5	aripiprazole was associated with gradual weight restoration and a reduction in distress around eating, obsesssional thoughts about food, weight and body image, and eating-disordered behaviors, and some improvements in depression, generalized anxiety, and cognitive flexibility

Study	Drug	Control	Study Design	Age of subjects	N	Outcome
Other (i.e., drugs in other classes, studies that include multiple classes of drugs)						
[23]	Amitriptyline (TCA)or Cypro-heptadine (weight-inducing drug)	placebo	randomized double-blind	adolescents adults	72	only cyproheptadine was associated with a decrease in the number of days necessary to achieve a normal weight, outcome differences in anorexia nervosa subtypes, and some improvement in depression
[75]	Cyproheptadine (weight-inducing drug)	placebo	controlled trial	not available	81	overall, cyproheptadine had no therapeutic benefit in the absence or presence of behavior therapy, except in some severe cases
[41]	Fluoxetine (SSRI), Fluvoxamine (SSRI), Sertraline(SSRI), Paroxetine (SSRI), or Clomipramine (TCA)	no SSRI	retrospective chart review	adolescents adults	40	drug treatment had no significant effect on clinical symptoms when administered in an inpatient setting
[44]	Olanzapine (AA) + Mirtazapine (TeCA)	none	case report	adult	1	combined treatment of olanzapine and mirtazapine was associated with improvements in symptoms
[52]	Olanzapine (AA) + Fluoxetine (SSRI) + Alprazolam (benzodiazepine)	none	case report	adolescent	1	olanzapine was associated with weight gain and improvement in psychological symptoms
[63]	Olanzapine (AA) or Chlorpro-mazine (TA)	none	randomized	adolescents adults	15	olanzapine was associated with a reduction in anorexic rumination
[71]	Amisulpride (AA), Fluoxetine (SSRI), or Clomipramine (TCA)	none	single-blind	adults	35	amisulpride was associated with a more significant increase in weight
[76]	Olanzapine (AA)+ Paroxetine (SSRI)	none	case study	adolescent	1	combined treatment was associated with complete symptom remission when combined with individual and family psychotherapy

*An older version of this table has been previously published [9]. Permission to publish an updated version for this chapter has been granted by Bentham Science Publishers.

This chapter will review the current status of pharmacological treatments for anorexia nervosa. An overview of studies is provided in Table 1. A wide variety of drugs have been utilized in the treatment of anorexia nervosa, including typical antipsychotics, tricyclic antidepressants, selective serotonin reuptake inhibitors, tetracyclic antidepressants, and atypical antipsychotics, and the results from these studies will be reviewed here. Several other compounds have also been examined in the treatment of anorexia nervosa, for example, antihistamines, prokinetic agents, zinc, lithium, naltrexone, growth hormone, and delta-9-tetrahydrocannabiol and the results from these studies have been reviewed elsewhere [10].

Typical Antipsychotics

Typical antipsychotics exert their mechanism of action through multiple neurotransmitter systems, particularly dopamine. Many typical antipsychotics are known to promote weight gain in non-eating disordered psychiatric populations, as well as improve psychiatric symptoms, thereby providing a rationale for administering these drugs to individuals with anorexia nervosa. The limited number of studies that have utilized typical antipsychotics in the treatment of anorexia nervosa have demonstrated few promising results. In one study, the combined use of chlorpromazine and insulin was associated with an initial increase in weight gain during inpatient hospitalization, but had no effect on long-term outcome [15]. In an open trial of pimozide, there was no significant effect on outcome when combined with behavior therapy [16], whereas a double-blind, placebo-controlled cross-over analysis of pimozide and behavior therapy was associated with an improved attitude towards treatment in a small sample of individuals [17]. In a double-blind, placebo-controlled, crossover analysis, sulpiride was associated with an early effect on weight gain, however, cross over analysis did not reach statistical significance [18]. In an open trial, haloperidol was associated with some improvements in body weight and eating disorder subscales when used as an adjunct to standard eating disorders treatment, but a larger, controlled study is needed to confirm these findings [19]. Overall, limited evidence from published studies, as well as a lack of large, controlled trials using typical antipsychotics, suggests there is no evidence to support the use of these drugs in the treatment of anorexia nervosa.

Tricyclic Antidepressants (TCAs)

The mechanism of action of TCAs occurs through inhibition of norepinephrine and serotonin reuptake into central nerve terminals, resulting in increased concentrations of these neurotransmitters at receptor sites. In a randomized, double-blind, placebo-controlled trial, clomipramine was associated with increased hunger, appetite, and energy intake, but was also associated with a reduced rate of weight gain during inpatient treatment [20], whereas a second study found no impact on outcome at the end of treatment [21]. In a double-blind, placebo-controlled trial, amytriptyline had no signifycant effect on outcome in the treatment of anorexia nervosa compared to placebo or psychosocial treatment alone and was associated with substantial discomfort and adverse effects [22]. In a randomized, double-blind trial of amitriptyline and cyproheptadine (a weight-inducing drug), only cyproheptadine was associated with a marginal effect on decreasing the number of days necessary to reach a normal weight and on depressive symptoms [23]. Overall, limited evidence from published studies, as well as a lack of large, controlled trials using TCAs, suggests there is no evidence to support the use of these drugs in the treatment of anorexia nervosa.

Selective Serotonin Reuptake Inhibitors (SSRIs)

The mechanism of action of SSRIs occurs via potentiation of serotonin by inhibition of its neuronal reuptake pump and desensitization of the serotonin 5-HT_{1A} receptor. Given the high rates of comorbidity with depression and anxiety disorders in anorexia nervosa (for example, [12, 13]), and the profound disturbances in the serotonin neurotransmitter system found during the acute phase of illness and following long-term recovery (for review see Chapter 6 and [24, 25]), the use of SSRIs for the treatment of anorexia nervosa would appear to be well justified. Unfortunately, initial positive findings supporting the use of SSRIs in the treatment of anorexia nervosa have not held up in larger, controlled studies.

Fluoxetine is the most widely studied SSRI in the treatment of anorexia nervosa. In an early case report of fluoxetine treatment in an individual with chronic anorexia nervosa, the drug was associated with improvements in weight, mood, and eating disorder symptomatology [26]. In one open trial, fluoxetine was associated with an improvement in depressive symptoms and subsequent weight gain [27], whereas another study comparing drug-treated individuals to matched historical case-controls showed no additive or synergistic therapeutic benefit to adding fluoxetine to inpatient treatment [28]. In a randomized, double-blind, placebo-controlled trial of fluoxetine during inpatient treatment, there were no significant differences on any measure between drug and placebo treatment groups [29]. In a study of nutritional management with and without fluoxetine augmentation, fluoxetine was associated with an earlier and significantly greater increase in BMI compared to the non-drug treated group, as well as a significant decrease in physical exercise [30]. The lack of conclusive evidence supporting the use of fluoxetine in the treatment of anorexia nervosa and in improving comorbid symptoms of depression and anxiety has raised the possibility that severe deficits in nutritional status may influence drug pharmacology; however, a double-blind, placebo-controlled trial of fluoxetine plus nutritional supplements failed to provide support for this hypothesis, as nutritional supplements did not increase the efficacy of fluoxetine when administered during the acute phase of anorexia nervosa [31].

When fluoxetine was administered after weight restoration in anorexia nervosa, one open trial found that fluoxetine was associated with weight maintenance over time [32]. In a prospective longitudinal follow-up of individuals on fluoxetine compared to matched historical controls, fluoxetine had no significant effect on the cumulative probability of remaining at target weight during the follow-up period, the risk of sustained weight loss, or other clinical measures of outcome [33]. In a double-blind, placebo-controlled trial of fluoxetine administered to weight restored patients after inpatient discharge, fluoxetine was associated with reduced relapse as determined by a significant increase in weight and a reduction in symptoms [34]. Despite this positive initial finding, a second, randomized, double-blind, placebo-controlled trial failed to find any difference between fluoxetine and placebo in time-to-relapse when administered after inpatient weight restoration [35].

In open trials of the SSRI citalopram, drug treatment has been associated with some improvement in weight and symptoms [36], as well as some improvements in body image dissatisfaction when combined with systemic psychotherapy [37]. In a randomized study of citalopram and wait-listed controls, citalopram was associated with improvements in depression, obsessive-compulsive symptoms, impulsiveness, and trait-anger, but no difference in weight gain during outpatient treatment [38]. In a retrospective case analysis comparing adjunctive SSRI treatment (fluoxetine, fluvoxamine, or sertraline) or no SSRI treatment during inpatient treatment and follow-up, there were no significant differences between drug and non-drug groups on rates of readmissions, BMI, core eating disorder symptoms, depression, or obsessive-compulsive scores [39]. In a controlled trial of venlafaxine and fluoxetine plus cognitive behavioral therapy in individuals with atypical anorexia nervosa, both drugs were associated with an increase in BMI and a significant reduction of eating disorder symptoms and depression scores, whereas venlafaxine was also associated with a reduction in anxiety [40]. In a retrospective chart review of inpatients with anorexia nervosa, supplemental SSRI medication (fluoxetine, fluvoxamine, sertraline, or paroxetine, or the TCA clomipramine) had no benefit above inpatient treatment alone on clinical symptoms [41]. Case reports of sertraline showed some effects on body weight and symptoms [42], whereas an open trial was associated with a reduction of depressive symptoms, perfectionist attitudes, ineffectiveness, and a lack of interoceptive awareness, but no effect on weight [43]. Overall, the limited number of studies and inconsistent findings across published studies of SSRIs suggests there is no evidence to support the use of these drugs in the treatment of anorexia nervosa.

Tetracyclic Antidepressants (TeCA)

The mechanism of action of TeCAs occurs primarily through inhibition of serotonin and norepinephrine reuptake. In two case reports mirtazapine was associated with weight gain and improvements in depression [44, 45]. In a case-control design, there were no significant differences between mirtazapine treated and matched controls with regard to weight gain or BMI during hospitalization, however, there was a non-significant trend in several other measures in the mirtazapine-treated group [46]. Overall, limited evidence from published studies, as well as a lack of large, controlled trials using TeCAs, suggests there is no evidence to support the use of these drugs in the treatment of anorexia nervosa.

Atypical Antipsychotics

Currently, the most promising class of drugs for the treatment of anorexia nervosa is the atypical antipsychotics. The mechanism of action of atypical antipsychotics is broad and varies across specific drugs, however, most compounds in this class exert their action through a combination of effects on serotonin and dopamine receptors. Olanzapine, a drug known to promote weight gain in other psychiatric populations, has been the most widely studied atypical antipsychotic in the treatment of anorexia nervosa. In several case reports and open trials, olanzapine has been associated with a number of effects, including reductions in depression, anxiety, obsessive compulsive symptoms, eating disorder symptoms, agitation, resistance to treatment, and/or activity levels as well as improvements in weight gain and/or maintenance [47-58]. In a double-blind, placebo-controlled trial, olanzapine plus cognitive behavioral therapy was associated with improvements in numerous aspects of treatment with some differences between subtypes of anorexia nervosa [59], whereas a second study in individuals undergoing day hospital treatment found augmentation with olanzapine was associated with a greater rate of weight gain, earlier achievement of target body mass index, and a greater rate of decrease in obsessive symptoms [60]. Two other double blind, placebo-controlled studies failed to find an effect of adding olanzapine to either cognitive-behavioral psychotherapy and programmed nutritional rehabilitation [61] or a comprehensive eating disorders treatment program [62]. A randomized trial of olanzapine versus the antipsychotic chlorpromazine found that only olanzapine was associated with a reduction in anorexic rumination [63]. Although some contradictory evidence exists, the overall positive findings of olanzapine in the treatment of anorexia nervosa warrants further investigation.

In case reports, risperidone was associated with an improvement in body weight and symptoms [64, 65], however, in a double-blind, placebo-controlled trial, there was no benefit to adding risperidone during the weight restoration phase of care in an eating disorders program [66]. Case reports and open trials have provided some evidence for the use of quetiapine to improve eating and/or psychopathological symptoms, such as depression, anxiety, and/or obsessive compulsive symptoms [67-69]. In a randomized trial of quetiapine versus treatment as usual, drug treatment was associated with a trend towards both psychological and physical improvements [70]. In a single-blind trial comparing amisulpride to fluoxetine (SSRI) and clomipramine (TCA), amisulpride was associated with a more significant increase in weight compared to the other drugs [71]. Finally, recent case reports on the use of aripiprazole as an adjunct to treatment found that aripiprazole was associated with gradual weight restoration and a reduction in distress around eating, obsessional thoughts about food, weight and body image, and eating-disordered behaviors, as well as some improvements in depression, generalized anxiety, and cognitive flexibility [72].

Across the atypical antipsychotics, olanzapine has shown the most promising effects when used as an adjunct to other treatments, with some preliminary evidence arising for the newer drugs. This class of drug clearly warrants further investigation for use in the treatment of anorexia nervosa.

Discussion

While the use of pharmacological treatments for anorexia nervosa often appears promising in case reports and open trials, the majority of findings have not been replicated in double-blind, placebo-controlled trials. The World Federation of Societies of Biology Psychiatry recently published guidelines for the pharmacological treatment of eating disorders [10]. The authors of this task force concluded that there was Grade B evidence (indicating limited positive evidence from controlled studies) for the use of olanzapine in promoting weight gain in anorexia nervosa and Grade C evidence (indicating positive evidence from uncontrolled studies or case reports/expert opinion) for other atypical antipsychotics when these drugs are used as an adjunct to other treatments [10]. Overall, there was no evidence for the general use of typical antipsychotics or antidepressants in the treatment of anorexia nervosa. Clearly, additional research is needed to identify the biological systems driving the unrelenting self-starvation (and often hyperactivity) in individuals with anorexia nervosa in order to develop more targeted pharmacological treatments for this deadly disease.

References

[1] Strober M, Freeman R, Morrell W. (1997). The long-term course of severe anorexia nervosa in adolescents: survival analysis of recovery, relapse, and outcome predictors over 10-15 years in a prospective study. *Int J Eat Disord, 22*:339-60.

[2] Lowe B, Zipfel S, Buchholz C, Dupont Y, Reas DL, Herzog W. (2001). Long-term outcome of anorexia nervosa in a prospective 21-year follow-up study. *Psychol Med, 31*:881-90.

[3] Steinhausen HC. (2002). The outcome of anorexia nervosa in the 20th century. *Am J Psychiatry, 159*:1284-93.

[4] Fisher M. (2003). The course and outcome of eating disorders in adults and in adolescents: a review. *Adolesc Med, 14*:149-58.

[5] Eddy KT, Dorer DJ, Franko DL, Tahilani K, Thompson-Brenner H, Herzog DB. (2008). Diagnostic crossover in anorexia nervosa and bulimia nervosa: implications for DSM-V. *Am J Psychiatry, 165*:245-50.

[6] Sullivan PF. (1995). Mortality in anorexia nervosa. *Am J Psychiatry, 152*:1073-4.

[7] Birmingham CL, Su J, Hlynsky JA, Goldner EM, Gao M. (2005). The mortality rate from anorexia nervosa. *Int J Eat Disord, 38*:143-6.

[8] Bulik CM, Berkman ND, Brownley KA, Sedway JA, Lohr KN. (2007). Anorexia nervosa treatment: a systematic review of randomized controlled trials. *Int J Eat Disord, 40*:310-20.

[9] Barbarich-Marsteller NC. (2007). Neurochemistry and pharmacological treatments: Where is the field of anorexia nervosa heading? *Central Nervous System Agents in Medicinal Chemistry, 7*:35-43.

[10] Aigner M, Treasure J, Kaye W, Kasper S. (2011). World Federation of Societies of Biological Psychiatry (WFSBP) Guidelines for the Pharmacological Treatment of Eating Disorders. *World J Biol Psychiatry, 12*:400-43.

[11] Zhu AJ, Walsh BT. (2002). Pharmacologic treatment of eating disorders. *Can J Psychiatry, 47*:227-34.

[12] Kaye WH, Bulik CM, Thornton L, Barbarich N, Masters K. (2004). Comorbidity of anxiety disorders with anorexia and bulimia nervosa. *Am J Psychiatry, 161*:2215-21.

[13] Fernandez-Aranda F, Pinheiro AP, Tozzi F, Thornton LM, Fichter MM, Halmi KA, et al. (2007). Symptom profile of major depressive disorder in women with eating disorders. *Aust N Z J Psychiatry, 41*:24-31.

[14] Walsh BT, Devlin MJ. (1998). Eating disorders: progress and problems. *Science, 280*:1387-90.

[15] Dally P, Sargant W. (1966). Treatment and outcome of anorexia nervosa. *Br Med J, 2*:793-5.

[16] Weizman A, Tyano S, Wijsenbeek H, Ben David M. (1985). Behavior therapy, pimozide treatment and prolactin secretion in anorexia nervosa. *Psychother Psychosom, 43*:136-40.

[17] Vandereycken W, Pierloot R. (1982). Pimozide combined with behavior therapy in the short-term treatment of anorexia nervosa. A double-blind placebo-controlled cross-over study. *Acta Psychiatr Scand, 66*:445-50.

[18] Vandereycken W. (1984). Neuroleptics in the short-term treatment of anorexia nervosa. A double-blind placebo-controlled study with sulpiride. *Br J Psychiatry, 144*:288-92.

[19] Cassano GB, Miniati M, Pini S, Rotondo A, Banti S, Borri C, et al. (2003). Six-month open trial of haloperidol as an adjunctive treatment for anorexia nervosa: a preliminary report. *Int J Eat Disord, 33*:172-7.
[20] Lacey JH, Crisp AH. (1980). Hunger, food intake and weight: the impact of clomipramine on a refeeding anorexia nervosa population. *Postgrad Med J, 56 Suppl 1*:79-85.
[21] Crisp AH, Lacey JH, Crutchfield M. (1987). Clomipramine and 'drive' in people with anorexia nervosa: an in-patient study. *Br J Psychiatry, 150*:355-8.
[22] Biederman J, Herzog DB, Rivinus TM, Harper GP, Ferber RA, Rosenbaum JF, et al. (1985). Amitriptyline in the treatment of anorexia nervosa: a double-blind, placebo-controlled study. *J Clin Psychopharmacol, 5*:10-6.
[23] Halmi KA, Eckert E, LaDu TJ, Cohen J. (1986). Anorexia nervosa. Treatment efficacy of cyproheptadine and amitriptyline. *Arch Gen Psychiatry, 43*:177-81.
[24] Kaye W. (2008). Neurobiology of anorexia and bulimia nervosa. *Physiol Behav, 94*:121-35.
[25] Kaye WH, Bailer UF, Frank GK, Wagner A, Henry SE. (2005). Brain imaging of serotonin after recovery from anorexia and bulimia nervosa. *Physiol Behav, 86*:15-7.
[26] Ferguson JM. (1987). Treatment of an anorexia nervosa patient with fluoxetine. *Am J Psychiatry, 144*:1239.
[27] Gwirtsman HE, Guze BH, Yager J, Gainsley B. (1990). Fluoxetine treatment of anorexia nervosa: an open clinical trial. *J Clin Psychiatry, 51*:378-82.
[28] Strober M, Pataki C, Freeman R, DeAntonio M. (1999). No effect of adjunctive fluoxetine on eating behavior or weight phobia during the inpatient treatment of anorexia nervosa: an historical case-control study. *J Child Adolesc Psychopharmacol, 9*:195-201.
[29] Attia E, Haiman C, Walsh BT, Flater SR. (1998). Does fluoxetine augment the inpatient treatment of anorexia nervosa? *Am J Psychiatry, 155*:548-51.
[30] Ruggiero GM, Mauri MC, Omboni AC, Volonteri LS, Dipasquale S, Malvini L, et al. (2003). Nutritional management of anorexic patients with and without fluoxetine: 1-year follow-up. *Prog Neuropsychopharmacol Biol Psychiatry, 27*:425-30.
[31] Barbarich NC, McConaha CW, Halmi KA, Gendall K, Sunday SR, Gaskill J, et al. (2004). Use of nutritional supplements to increase the

efficacy of fluoxetine in the treatment of anorexia nervosa. *Int J Eat Disord, 35*:10-5.

[32] Kaye WH, Weltzin TE, Hsu LK, Bulik CM. (1991). An open trial of fluoxetine in patients with anorexia nervosa. *J Clin Psychiatry, 52*:464-71.

[33] Strober M, Freeman R, DeAntonio M, Lampert C, Diamond J. (1997). Does adjunctive fluoxetine influence the post-hospital course of restrictor-type anorexia nervosa? A 24-month prospective, longitudinal followup and comparison with historical controls. *Psychopharmacol Bull, 33*:425-31.

[34] Kaye WH, Nagata T, Weltzin TE, Hsu LK, Sokol MS, McConaha C, et al. (2001). Double-blind placebo-controlled administration of fluoxetine in restricting- and restricting-purging-type anorexia nervosa. *Biol Psychiatry, 49*:644-52.

[35] Walsh BT, Kaplan AS, Attia E, Olmsted M, Parides M, Carter JC, et al. (2006). Fluoxetine after weight restoration in anorexia nervosa: a randomized controlled trial. *JAMA, 295*:2605-12.

[36] Pallanti S, Quercioli L, Ramacciotti A. (1997). Citalopram in anorexia nervosa. *Eat Weight Disord, 2*:216-21.

[37] Calandra C, Gulino V, Inserra L, Giuffrida A. (1999). The use of citalopram in an integrated approach to the treatment of eating disorders: an open study. *Eat Weight Disord, 4*:207-10.

[38] Fassino S, Leombruni P, Daga G, Brustolin A, Migliaretti G, Cavallo F, et al. (2002). Efficacy of citalopram in anorexia nervosa: a pilot study. *Eur Neuropsychopharmacol, 12*:453-9.

[39] Holtkamp K, Konrad K, Kaiser N, Ploenes Y, Heussen N, Grzella I, et al. (2005). A retrospective study of SSRI treatment in adolescent anorexia nervosa: insufficient evidence for efficacy. *J Psychiatr Res, 39*:303-10.

[40] Ricca V, Mannucci E, Paionni A, Di Bernardo M, Cellini M, Cabras PL, et al. (1999). Venlafaxine versus fluoxetine in the treatment of atypical anorectic outpatients: a preliminary study. *Eat Weight Disord, 4*:10-4.

[41] Ferguson CP, La Via MC, Crossan PJ, Kaye WH. (1999). Are serotonin selective reuptake inhibitors effective in underweight anorexia nervosa? *Int J Eat Disord, 25*:11-7.

[42] Frank GK, Kaye WH, Marcus MD. (2001). Sertraline in underweight binge eating/purging-type eating disorders: five case reports. *Int J Eat Disord, 29*:495-8.

[43] Santonastaso P, Friederici S, Favaro A. (2001). Sertraline in the treatment of restricting anorexia nervosa: an open controlled trial. *J Child Adolesc Psychopharmacol, 11*:143-50.

[44] Wang TS, Chou YH, Shiah IS. (2006). Combined treatment of olanzapine and mirtazapine in anorexia nervosa associated with major depression. *Prog Neuropsychopharmacol Biol Psychiatry, 30*:306-9.

[45] Safer DL, Darcy AM, Lock J. (2011). Use of mirtazapine in an adult with refractory anorexia nervosa and comorbid depression: a case report. *Int J Eat Disord, 44*:178-81.

[46] Hrdlicka M, Beranova I, Zamecnikova R, Urbanek T. (2008). Mirtazapine in the treatment of adolescent anorexia nervosa. Case-control study. *Eur Child Adolesc Psychiatry, 17*:187-9.

[47] Jensen VS, Mejlhede A. (2000). Anorexia nervosa: treatment with olanzapine. *Br J Psychiatry, 177*:87.

[48] La Via MC, Gray N, Kaye WH. (2000). Case reports of olanzapine treatment of anorexia nervosa. *Int J Eat Disord, 27*:363-6.

[49] Mehler C, Wewetzer C, Schulze U, Warnke A, Theisen F, Dittmann RW. (2001). Olanzapine in children and adolescents with chronic anorexia nervosa. A study of five cases. *Eur Child Adolesc Psychiatry, 10*:151-7.

[50] Powers PS, Santana CA, Bannon YS. (2002). Olanzapine in the treatment of anorexia nervosa: an open label trial. *Int J Eat Disord, 32*:146-54.

[51] Bosanac P, Burrows G, Norman T. (2003). Olanzapine in anorexia nervosa. *Aust N Z J Psychiatry, 37*:494.

[52] Ercan ES, Copkunol H, Cykoethlu S, Varan A. (2003). Olanzapine treatment of an adolescent girl with anorexia nervosa. *Hum Psychopharmacol, 18*:401-3.

[53] Boachie A, Goldfield GS, Spettigue W. (2003). Olanzapine use as an adjunctive treatment for hospitalized children with anorexia nervosa: case reports. *Int J Eat Disord, 33*:98-103.

[54] Malina A, Gaskill J, McConaha C, Frank GK, LaVia M, Scholar L, et al. (2003). Olanzapine treatment of anorexia nervosa: a retrospective study. *Int J Eat Disord, 33*:234-7.

[55] Barbarich NC, McConaha CW, Gaskill J, La Via M, Frank GK, Achenbach S, et al. (2004). An open trial of olanzapine in anorexia nervosa. *J Clin Psychiatry, 65*:1480-2.

[56] Hillebrand JJ, van Elburg AA, Kas MJ, van Engeland H, Adan RA. (2005). Olanzapine reduces physical activity in rats exposed to activity-

based anorexia: possible implications for treatment of anorexia nervosa? *Biol Psychiatry, 58*:651-7.

[57] Dennis K, Le Grange D, Bremer J. (2006). Olanzapine use in adolescent anorexia nervosa. *Eat Weight Disord, 11*:e53-6.

[58] Leggero C, Masi G, Brunori E, Calderoni S, Carissimo R, Maestro S, et al. (2010). Low-dose olanzapine monotherapy in girls with anorexia nervosa, restricting subtype: focus on hyperactivity. *J Child Adolesc Psychopharmacol, 20*:127-33.

[59] Brambilla F, Garcia CS, Fassino S, Daga GA, Favaro A, Santonastaso P, et al. (2007). Olanzapine therapy in anorexia nervosa: psychobiological effects. *Int Clin Psychopharmacol, 22*:197-204.

[60] Bissada H, Tasca GA, Barber AM, Bradwejn J. (2008). Olanzapine in the treatment of low body weight and obsessive thinking in women with anorexia nervosa: a randomized, double-blind, placebo-controlled trial. *Am J Psychiatry, 165*:1281-8.

[61] Brambilla F, Monteleone P, Maj M. (2007). Olanzapine-induced weight gain in anorexia nervosa: involvement of leptin and ghrelin secretion? *Psychoneuroendocrinology, 32*:402-6.

[62] Kafantaris V, Leigh E, Hertz S, Berest A, Schebendach J, Sterling WM, et al. (2011). A placebo-controlled pilot study of adjunctive olanzapine for adolescents with anorexia nervosa. *J Child Adolesc Psychopharmacol, 21*:207-12.

[63] Mondraty N, Birmingham CL, Touyz S, Sundakov V, Chapman L, Beumont P. (2005). Randomized controlled trial of olanzapine in the treatment of cognitions in anorexia nervosa. *Australas Psychiatry, 13*:72-5.

[64] Fisman S, Steele M, Short J, Byrne T, Lavallee C. (1996). Case study: anorexia nervosa and autistic disorder in an adolescent girl. *J Am Acad Child Adolesc Psychiatry, 35*:937-40.

[65] Newman-Toker J. (2000). Risperidone in anorexia nervosa. *J Am Acad Child Adolesc Psychiatry, 39*:941-2.

[66] Hagman J, Gralla J, Sigel E, Ellert S, Dodge M, Gardner R, et al. (2011). A double-blind, placebo-controlled study of risperidone for the treatment of adolescents and young adults with anorexia nervosa: a pilot study. *J Am Acad Child Adolesc Psychiatry, 50*:915-24.

[67] Bosanac P, Kurlender S, Norman T, Hallam K, Wesnes K, Manktelow T, et al. (2007). An open-label study of quetiapine in anorexia nervosa. *Hum Psychopharmacol, 22*:223-30.

[68] Powers PS, Bannon Y, Eubanks R, McCormick T. (2007). Quetiapine in anorexia nervosa patients: an open label outpatient pilot study. *Int J Eat Disord, 40*:21-6.
[69] Mehler-Wex C, Romanos M, Kirchheiner J, Schulze UM. (2008). Atypical antipsychotics in severe anorexia nervosa in children and adolescents--review and case reports. *Eur Eat Disord Rev, 16*:100-8.
[70] Court A, Mulder C, Kerr M, Yuen HP, Boasman M, Goldstone S, et al. (2010). Investigating the effectiveness, safety and tolerability of quetiapine in the treatment of anorexia nervosa in young people: a pilot study. *J Psychiatr Res, 44*:1027-34.
[71] Ruggiero GM, Laini V, Mauri MC, Ferrari VM, Clemente A, Lugo F, et al. (2001). A single blind comparison of amisulpride, fluoxetine and clomipramine in the treatment of restricting anorectics. *Prog Neuropsychopharmacol Biol Psychiatry, 25*:1049-59.
[72] Trunko ME, Schwartz TA, Duvvuri V, Kaye WH. (2011). Aripiprazole in anorexia nervosa and low-weight bulimia nervosa: case reports. *Int J Eat Disord, 44*:269-75.
[73] Spettigue W, Buchholz A, Henderson K, Feder S, Moher D, Kourad K, et al. (2008). Evaluation of the efficacy and safety of olanzapine as an adjunctive treatment for anorexia nervosa in adolescent females: a randomized, double-blind, placebo-controlled trial. *BMC Pediatr, 8*:4.
[74] Norris ML, Spettigue W, Buchholz A, Henderson KA, Gomez R, Maras D, et al. (2011). Olanzapine use for the adjunctive treatment of adolescents with anorexia nervosa. *J Child Adolesc Psychopharmacol, 21*:213-20.
[75] Goldberg SC, Halmi KA, Eckert ED, Casper RC, Davis JM. (1979). Cyproheptadine in anorexia nervosa. *Br J Psychiatry, 134*:67-70.
[76] Dadic-Hero E, Ruzic K, Pernar M, Kabalin M, Medved P. (2009). Olanzapine treatment in anorexia nervosa: case report. *Psychiatr Danub, 21*:122-5.

In: Anorexia Nervosa
Editor: N. C. Barbarich-Marsteller

ISBN: 978-1-62081-291-4

Chapter 6

Insights From Brain Imaging Studies in Anorexia Nervosa

Guido K. W. Frank* and Lisa N. Mettler
Colorado Children's Hospital, University of Colorado Anschutz Medical Campus, School of Medicine, Department of Psychiatry, Aurora, CO, US

Abstract

Anorexia nervosa (AN) is a severe psychiatric disorder that is associated with abnormalities of brain structure and function. There are a variety of brain imaging techniques that have been used to study AN giving us new insights into altered brain function in this disorder that could be related to pathologic behavior. For instance, radioligand imaging could identify alterations in brain neurotransmitter function, and studies using tasks that apply food or body image related stimuli could elicit altered response in fear or reward circuitry. In this chapter we review the available literature on the various findings and how such alterations may be related to the pathophysiology of the disorder.

* Corresponding Author: Guido K.W. Frank, M.D., Assistant Professor in Child and Adolescent Psychiatry, Developmental Brain Research Program, Department of Psychiatry, University of Colorado at Denver and Health Sciences Center, The Children's Hospital, Gary Pavilion A036/B-130, 13123 East 16th Avenue, Aurora, CO 80045, Tel.: 720-777-1909

INTRODUCTION

AN is an eating disorder that usually begins during adolescence, most commonly in females, and is associated with an intense fear of gaining weight, feeling fat despite being underweight, emaciation, and amenorrhea. The hallmark sign of low weight is defined as a body mass index (BMI, weight in kilograms / height in meters^2) of <17.5. A restricting type (AN-R), marked by food restriction and usually over-exercising, has been distinguished from a binge-eating/purging type (AN-B/P), where afflicted individuals regularly overeat and then use measures such as self induced vomiting, laxatives or diuretics in order to lose or not gain weight [1]. Comorbid depression and anxiety disorders are common [2].

The conceptual framework of the pathophysiology and etiology of AN has substantially developed over the past few decades. Brain imaging techniques now give us the opportunity to assess regional brain activity and neuroreceptor function *in vivo* in humans, and thus may help us understand how neuronal circuits are related to behavior and pathophysiology.

The neuroimaging tools available include structural imaging techniques such as computer tomography (CT) and radiation-free magnetic resonance imaging (MRI) that provide information on gross structural abnormalities. Magnetic resonance spectroscopy (MRS) can detect brain chemicals containing choline, aspartate and others, which are involved in brain neurotransmission. Positron emission tomography (PET), single photon emission computed tomography (SPECT), and functional magnetic resonance imaging (fMRI) are used to assess brain activity thought to be associated with changes in regional cerebral blood flow (rCBF). In addition, neurotransmitter receptor function and regional cerebral glucose metabolism (rCGM) can be assessed with PET and SPECT together with radio-ligands. Electroencephalography (EEG) and evoked potentials (EPs) record neuronal electrical activity, and quantitative electroencephalography (qEEG) employs spectral analysis of EEG data from multiple-electrode, whole-head recordings, providing better spatial resolution compared to the traditional EEG.Recent advances in the field of brain research using neuroscience-based imaging paradigms have made great progress with respect to emotional and cognitive processes that may be altered in psychiatric illness. For example, a lot has been learned about brain pathways that are involved in fear provoking stimuli [3], induction of abnormal mood states [4], processing of food and other rewarding stimuli [5], cognitive flexibility [6], and numerous other areas with potential relevance to AN. In comparison with, for instance, psychosis or depression research, the body of neurobiologic research in AN is small, but nevertheless significant advances have been made over the past ten years to shed light on biological brain processes that may be part of the pathophysiology of AN.

The ill state of AN can be accompanied by severe metabolic, electrolyte, and endocrine disturbances [1]. As such, research in AN is always potentially confounded by these effects. On the other hand, research in recovered subjects could represent either premorbid traits contributing to the development of the illness, or a consequence of having been previously ill and thus not directly reflecting risk factors or problems during the ill state. Consequently, these factors have to be taken into consideration when reviewing the literature.

CT AND MRI STUDIES

CT and MRI studies generally show that underweight AN individuals tend to have enlarged sulci and ventricles and decreased brain mass [7-9]. While these alterations shift towards normal with weight restoration it has been questioned to what extent they normalize [10, 11]. It is also not quite clear whether these changes during the ill state are primarily related to changes in grey (GM) or white matter (WM), or the extracellular space. Moreover, it remains uncertain whether these are generalized brain changes or are specific to particular brain regions. Katzman's group [12] found in 13 adolescent AN women reduced total GM and WM as well as enlarged cerebrospinal fluid (CSF) volume during the ill state. By contrast, in a cohort of ill AN and control women, Husain assessed the midsagittal plane acquired by MRI, finding reduced midbrain and thalamic size in AN, but no GM alterations [13]. Lambe compared 12 *recovered* AN (defined as BMI > 17.0 kg/ m^2, regular menses > 6 months)to 13 ill AN and 18 controls, and found that they had reduced GM and increased CSF volume compared to controls, but greater GM and smaller CSF space compared to ill AN [14]. Furthermore, a longitudinal study on 6 women studied during the ill state and after weight recovery (mean 16 months), showed that WM volume was recovered after weight recovery, but a GM deficit persisted as well as increased CSF space [15]. More recently, Mühlau demonstrated a modest decrease in global GM volume after recovery from AN (n=22) compared to controls [16]. In addition, there was a persistent significant decrease in anterior cingulate cortex (ACC) volume that correlated with past lowest body mass index. It could be possible that this finding represents a cortical injury due to a period of severe malnourishment, or alternatively a state of only partial recovery. An analysis of MRIs of 12 female and 6 male AN individuals, again found a persistent decrease in ACC volume after recovery, and furthermore, the degree to which ACC volume was restored with recovery was positively correlated with sustained remission from AN symptoms[17]. However, Wagner performed the so far largest study in recovered eating disorder subjects, including 30 AN (14 AN-R, 16 AN-B/P), and found no significant alterations in GM, WM, or CSF volumes [18]. Furthermore, most recently, a case series of 12 ill adolescent AN subjects again revealed global GM loss that at seven month follow-up had completely reversed [19]. Thus it appears that these volume abnormalities are likely state-related, and normalize with long term recovery. This a further supported by one of the largest studies to date that suggest at least partial normalization of brain structure with recovery [20].

The reason for even these transient changes in brain volume is also not known. Some data suggest that cortisol may contribute to brain alterations. Katzman[12] found that urinary free cortisol was positively correlated with CSF, but inversely with GM volume. AN patients are known to have increased CSF cortisol [21]. Thus it is possible that hypercortisolemia may play a role in reduced brain mass in ill AN, maybe through its catabolic or fluid-homeostatic effects [22]. On the other hand, reduced mesial temporal cortex (amygdalo-hippocampal complex) size in ill AN did not show a relationship with hormonal levels including urinary free cortisol in another study [23], questioning the effects of cortisol on brain structure in AN.

The question of whether alterations in brain mass contribute to cognitive or mood changes in ill AN has not been well studied. Kingston [24] combined structural imaging with psychological assessments (including anxiety, depression, attention, memory) in 46 AN inpatients before and after weight gain, compared to controls. No significant correlations were found, suggesting either no specificity of disturbance that can be related to specific behavior, or simply inefficient analysis methods. Similarly, Connan correlated hippocampal volume in ill AN with cognitive testing, and while finding a decrease in hippocampal volume in the AN group, found no correlation between cognitive performance and hippocampal volume loss [25].

In summary, these studies tend to indicate that during the ill state, a GM and probably WM volume loss or shrinkage occur that at least partially recover with weight restoration. These structural alterations are relatively non-specific, and behavioral correlates have not been discovered.

A relatively new technique is diffusion tensor imaging that takes advantage of MRI pulse sequences that can elicit water diffusion in the brain and provide insight into integrity of fiber tracts. In the so far only study available adult AN had reduced fiber integrity particular in the fimbria fornix, an outflux tract from the hippocampus/mesial temporal cortex region that connects to prefrontal as well as limbic and reward processing areas such as the striatum [26]. Importantly, this alteration was predictive of high harm avoidance in AN and could indicate a mechanism for pathologic anxiety in AN. However, those results need replication and further study.

MRS Studies

MRS can give information on nerve cell damage by assessing brain metabolites such as choline, N-acetyl-aspartate (NAA), phosphorus, and myo-inositol. MRS studies in juvenile AN found higher choline-containing compounds relative to total creatinine and lower ratios of NAA relative to choline in WM [27, 28]. Those changes were interpreted to indicate altered cell membrane turnover, as they were reversible with recovery [29]. Two studies [30, 31] showed reduced brain phospholipids that positively correlated with BMI, also suggesting a state-dependent phenomenon. The latter study also found BMI positively correlated with frontal cortex myo-inositol, which is a part of the serotonin (5HT) second messenger neurotransmission system [32] and could be consistent with reduced 5HT activity in ill AN[33]. Castro-Fornieles[19], in a longitudinal study, found state-dependent changes in NAA, glutamate/glutamine, and myo-inositol that again resolved with recovery from illness, further indicating that metabolic alterations are state-dependent and do not represent pathogenetic traits. These metabolic alterations are likely to be related to the neuronal insults suffered from starvation. Moreover, in a recent study by Joos[34], it was found that there was not a significant difference in the neurochemistry of the ACC between the AN patients and the control women, suggesting that only some AN individuals may have brain alterations in those measures of brain neurochemistry.

PET and SPECT Studies, Resting Condition

Most studies that have assessed "resting" brain activity in AN have used SPECT. Gordon found that 13 of 15 ill AN had unilateral temporal lobe hypoperfusion that persisted in the subjects studied after weight restoration [35]. Kuruoglu studied two ill AN with bilateral hypoperfusion in frontal, temporal, and parietal regions which normalized after three months of remission [36]. Takano found hypoperfusion in 14 ill AN subjects in the medial prefrontal cortex and ACC, and hyperperfusion in the thalamus and amygdalo-hippocampal complex [37]. In a study by Chowdhury, 15 ill adolescent AN subjects had unilateral temporo-parietal and frontal lobe hypoperfusion [38], and Rastam found temporo-parietal and orbitofrontal hypoperfusion in ill and recovered AN subjects [39]. These studies, demonstrating mostly reduced rCBF in ill AN have, however, been challenged by a recent study that found no such abnormality when a partial volume correction, i.e. a correction for brain volume reduction seen in ill AN, was applied during image processing [40]. This is in contrast to the previous rCBF studies, and suggests that prior findings of reduced rCBF in AN could have been a confounded result due to brain volumetric alterations in AN [12]. After weight recovery however, Kojima demonstrated a decrease in rCBF in the ACC among 12 AN-R subjects [41]. Matsumoto studied 3 AN-R and 5 AN-B/P before and after weight recovery, finding increases in rCBF in several regions after inpatient treatment [42].The same study found a significant correlation between low interoceptive awareness score on Eating Disorders Inventory-3 (EDI-3) and decreased perfusion of right dorsolateral prefrontal cortex, which is implicated in emotional self-awareness, a trait that has long been proposed as abnormal in AN [43]. After long-term recovery, Frank [44] found no persistent alterations in cerebral perfusion in 10 recovered AN-R and 9 recovered AN-B/P subjects, indicating that such abnormalities in fact do recover with illness remission.

Fewer studies have assessed glucose metabolism using PET. Delvenne studied 20 ill AN who showed frontal and parietal hypometabolism compared to controls, which normalized with weight gain [45-48]. But here too, no correction for brain volume changes was applied, and the results would need to be confirmed in a partial volume corrected sample of ill AN individuals.

Taken together, resting brain activity studies in AN most frequently suggest alterations of the temporal, parietal or cingulate cortex during the ill state, and a few studies suggest persistent alterations in those areas after weight gain. It remains unclear whether cerebral perfusion changes truly exist or are just a technical confound due to brain volume abnormalities. If there is in fact reduced rCBF or glucose metabolism in ill and recovered AN, that could be a potentially important finding given that the mesial temporal cortex is implicated in emotional processing, and increased anxiety in AN could be related to altered amygdala function. However, at this point reduced rCBF after recovery and even during the ill state may be less likely [49, 50].

A study by Yonezawa[51] compared ill AN-R and AN-B/P using SPECT, and found no significant differences in rCBF between the two groups, suggesting that cerebral blood flow is not part of pathophysiology that distinguishes the two AN subtypes. Interestingly, Goethals demonstrated an absence of rCBF differences between diagnoses among 31 AN-R, 16 AN-B/P, and 20 bulimics, but showed that among all diagnoses, rCBF results in prefrontal and parietal areas were positively correlated with measures of body dissatisfaction and ineffectiveness as measured by the Eating Disorders Inventory-3 (EDI-3) [52]. Taken together, resting brain activity so far is not a valid measure to distinguish AN subtypes, but could be related to eating disorder severity.

EEG, EPs, and qEEG

Eating disorders have been studied by EEG since at least 1955 [53].Since that time, much of the EEG work has focused on sleep and eating disorders. Early work confirmed the clinical finding that AN is accompanied by insomnia and early awakening [54, 55]. A complete overview of sleep EEG in AN is beyond the scope of this volume and we focus in this review on more specific AN related symptoms.

Evoked potentials (EPs), or event-related potentials (ERPs), are specific activations in time and location, generated by response to sensory stimuli, and measured by electrophysiologic recording. Variations in these activations' amplitudes provide evidence of the nature of cortical response to the associated stimuli. Bradley [56] engaged 20 ill AN adolescents in both a verbal and a nonverbal memory task, and found increased latency and decreased amplitude of the P300 activation, which is associated with attention, processing capacity and memory integration; this alteration suggests slowness and inefficiency in the memory task performance. In follow-up with 8 recovered AN, there was partial but incomplete improvement of this parameter compared to controls, suggesting the possibility of a memory-related cognitive processing impairment in AN apart from nutritional status. Another study (N = 12) used a sensory-filtering paradigm to assess P300 response to shape recognition. In controls, stimuli that appeared frequently would eventually yield a low-amplitude P300 response, suggestive of processing accommodation to repetition, however AN subjects showed a consistently elevated P300 response suggestive of hyperarousal[57]. Pieters[58] studied another ERP of interest, the error-related negativity, or ERN, which is a discrete drop in amplitude recorded following a response error, thought to be part of an error-monitoring mechanism to enhance learning. Among controls, "perfectionism," as a psychological trait measured by questionnaire, was correlated with a higher magnitude (more negative) ERN, as might be expected, during a simple visual processing task ("flankers task"). Among AN, perfectionism scores were higher, consistent with prior research [59], and AN subjects made fewer errors than their control counterparts. Paradoxically, however, AN showed a *weaker* ERN than did controls in the anterior cingulate cortex (ACC) area, when error rate was included as a covariate, suggesting less prominent error monitoring among AN subjects in the ACC. The significance of this surprising finding is unclear; the authors conjectured that AN may recruit other cerebral structures in their error monitoring, such that the activation measured by ERN is only part of their error-monitoring mechanism. Interestingly, fMRI studies have identified the ACC as the likely generator of the ERN signal [60, 61], and a number of fMRI studies have shown significant alterations in ACC activation in eating disorders. Pollatos[62] studied visual identification of emotional state of faces by 12 AN females, and their associated visual EPs (VEPs). This study found AN subjects performed worse than controls in the task of correctly identifying the emotional valence of the faces. The amplitude of the N200 VEP, which is associated with processing of unfamiliar stimuli, was increased in response to all emotional categories of faces. This may suggest that AN require more attentional resources in order to decode emotional states of others. The P300 response, on the other hand, was decreased in amplitude to faces with negative valence (fear, anger, disgust), but *increased* to neutral faces. The authors posit that this reflects AN subjects working harder to resolve the emotional valence of the more ambiguous condition, as representative of a possible disturbance in social cognition.

Quantitative EEG (qEEG) studies have recently come to prominence as another functional assessment method. A standard qEEG setup involves a 19-channel recording scheme with electrodes regularly distributed according to the International 10-20 system [63, 64]. Grunwald[63] gave ill AN subjects a tactile exploration task and measured theta-frequency band power on each hemisphere, finding an asymmetry in theta power in both resting and active states in ill AN but not in control women; furthermore, the active (but not resting) asymmetry persisted into recovery at follow-up testing. The significance of the global asymmetry is not obvious, but may reflect diffuse whole-hemispheric dysfunction in AN; the authors posit that this reflects a trait hyperarousal (leading to desynchronization and lower amplitude) of the right hemisphere. Alternatively, this finding may develop as a result of starvation and persist as a scar effect, with preferential preservation of the dominant left hemisphere function. The second qEEG study [65] included AN-R and AN-B/P subjects, who were not recovered but past the acute phase of the illness (5 to 47 days post hospital admission). That study found decreased alpha frequency power in central, parietal, occipital, and temporal/limbic areas. Loss of amplitude in the main arousal-related frequency bands (alpha, beta, theta) suggests synaptic dysfunction and neuronal damage [66-68]. The pathogenesis of the findings is unclear, but may be related in part to starvation, persistent electrolyte imbalance, and presence of psychotropic medication.

Task-Activation Studies using PET, SPECT, and fMRI

Functional brain imaging is performed in conjunction with paradigms and tasks that are meant to elicit areas of brain activation that might be specific for AN pathophysiology. Many different paradigms have been used over the past years, with PET and SPECT comprising the earlier work and fMRI achieving prominence more recently.

Eating custard cake showed increased brain activity in AN compared to controls using SPECT in frontal, occipital, parietal and temporal areas [69, 70]. Food imagination on SPECT showed that AN-B/P had greater right-sided parietal and prefrontal activation compared to controls and AN-R [71]. Gordon found, using PET, that in AN high-calorie foods provoked anxiety and led to greater temporo-occipital activation when compared to low calorie foods [72]. Ellison, using fMRI, also found that visual high calorie presentation elicited high anxiety in AN together with left mesial temporal as well as left insular and bilateral ACC activity [73]. These results could be consistent with anxiety provocation and related limbic activation [74]. Uher[75] used pictures of food and non-food aversive emotional stimuli to assess ill and recovered AN subjects. Food images stimulated medial prefrontal and ACC in both recovered and ill AN, but lateral prefrontal regions only in recovered AN; in controls food pictures were associated with occipital, basal ganglia and lateral prefrontal activation. Aversive non-food stimuli activated occipital and dorsolateral prefrontal cortex in all three subject-groups. In recovered AN, prefrontal cortex, ACC and cerebellum were more highly activated compared to both controls and chronic AN after food presentation. This suggested that higher ACC and medial prefrontal cortex activity in both ill and recovered AN compared to control women may be a trait marker for AN. These are areas of executive function, decision making, error monitoring and also reward expectancy. Such alterations could suggest heightened vigilance or processing activity in response to visual food stimuli. Taken together, these studies suggest that the prefrontal cortex is active in the capacity to appropriately or inappropriately restrict food, possibly via heightened fear related activation and anxious cognitions followed by related decision making such as food restriction. The amygdala, responsive to threat, could have an important role to trigger acquired food related fears and cognitions. In contrast to the above studies that tended to find increased cingulate activation in AN is a recent study using food images during fMRI [76] that found that the AN individuals showed a small area of hyperactivation in the amygdala, but reduced activation compared to controls in the cingulate cortex. However, the study used fairly low significance thresholds in addition to small sample sizes per group and the results need replication in a larger sample.

Santel[77] compared AN-R with control women confronted by food images in both hungry and satiated states. They noted a decrease in inferior parietal lobule (IPL) activation among satiated AN, and furthermore, the magnitude of decrease correlated with illness severity. The IPL is composed of both the primary somatosensory and sensory association cortices, so this finding suggests a decrease in sensory sensitivity, or increased habituation, to food images in ill AN, which could indicate a pathogenetic mechanism that facilitates fasting or restriction. In turn, in the hungry state, AN showed decreased activation to food stimuli in the occipital cortex compared to control women, which may indicate a learned or innate attentional bias away from food stimuli in the hungry state in AN, which again would facilitate fasting. A study by Gizewski[78] used food image exposure during the hungry and satiated states as well, but found that there was an increased activation of the prefrontal and central cortices, as well as the insula in the hungry state. In the satiated state increased activation was found in the left insula. That study indicated hyper-vigilance in the AN individuals to food stimuli in the hungry state in both primary taste cortex (insula) and executive function frontal cortex, but only in the taste cortex when satiated, suggesting an increased sensitivity to food stimuli, regardless of feeding state.

Neurophysiologic responses to taste stimuli are in the early stages of investigation. Wagner [79] used a 10% sucrose solution and water in recovered AN-R and found decreased ACC, insula, and striatal activation to both taste stimuli. Furthermore, self-report of pleasantness of the taste stimulus and activation in these brain regions were only correlated in controls. This suggests a possible difference in the processing of and habituation to tastes between AN-R and control women. The insula is implicated both in early processing of sensory stimuli as well as reward associations [80]. The ACC, as above, is implicated in reward anticipation and executive function [81]. It is an interesting contrast that the ACC in AN is activated by visual food stimuli in most studies, whereas its activation is decreased by gustatory stimuli in this study; this may represent a difference in stimulus saliency and anticipation versus actual stimulus-receipt processing. That is, while the food pictures tend to induce anxiety, individuals may learn to habituate or constrain their brain response. This brings up a major problem with these studies:when taste stimuli are expected, it is not clear what the impact of cognitive restraint may be with respect to reward activation control to expected and emotionally laden food stimuli. Along that hypothesis is a recent study [82] where AN individuals were given chocolate milk through a tube during an fMRI scan in a hungry valence as well as during a satiated state. It was observed that during the hunger state hyperactivation of the right amygdala and the left medial temporal gyrus occurred in response to the stimuli. This was hypothesized to perhaps represent vigilance to or fear of the food (therefore a fear of weight gain), and in the satiated state increased activation of the inferior temporal gyrus was observed, suggesting hypersensitivity. Another study found that recovered AN individuals had an increased activation of the ventral striatum and occipital cortex in response to pleasant taste and pleasant food images respectively; in response to aversive image and taste there was also an increased activation, compared to control women, of the anterior cingulate and caudate, and insula and putamen respectively [83]. These data may indicate that AN individuals quickly "shut down" their brain response when they are aware of the stimulus to be received, maybe in a form of cognitive restraint to control food intake. In contrast, when stimuli are received randomly, AN individuals show an excessive activation, potentially reflecting a hyper-sensitivity to salient stimuli [84].

Body image distortion is an integral part of AN pathophysiology and is part of its diagnostic criteria [1]. In a small pilot study confronting 3 AN subjects and 3 control women with their own digitally distorted body images using a computer-based video technique and fMRI [85], AN had greater activation in the brainstem, right sided amygdala and fusiform gyrus, again suggesting anxiety related to the body experience that is reflected by amygdala activity. However, in a follow up study in a larger and more homogeneous sample using the same paradigm, Wagner [86] found no amygdala activation but a hyper-responsiveness in brain areas belonging to the frontal visual system and the attention network (Brodmann area [BA] 9) as well as intraparietal lobule (IPL, BA 40), including the anterior part of the intraparietal sulcus. The latter areas are specifically involved in visuo-spatial processing. More broadly, the parietal lobes are implicated in body schema integration and body ownership [87]. This finding makes the involvement of the brain anxiety circuit less clear but suggests that perceptual alterations may be related directly to the mechanisms of body image construction. In comparison, a study in a group of control women only found left amygdala activation in relation to unpleasant body-related words, as well as contra-lateral parahippocampal activation that was negatively related to the Eating Disorders Inventory-2 (EDI-2) score [88]. The same group compared healthy control women with matched males in the same body-related word paradigm, and again found increased left amygdala activation among only the women, whereas the men showed increased activity in medial prefrontal cortex and hippocampus [88]. Thus young women, with or without AN, may have somewhat similar—probably learned—anxiety reactions to stimuli related to body image, which may help to explain in neurobiological terms why women are so much more susceptible to AN than men. In an fMRI study by Fladung[89] images of an underweight female body, a normal size body image, and overweight body image were used. It was found that AN individuals showed greater activation of the ventral striatal region during exposure to the underweight image, while CW showed greater activation of this region to the normal weight image. The activation of the reward system in response to underweight images may therefore reinforce a central symptom of AN, the desire to achieve a certain body type that is not considered desirable by non-AN women. Sachdev[90] studied brain response to images of self versus non-self in ill AN-R and AN-BP versus control women. That study found decreased activation in frontal, insula, precuneus and occipital regions for AN subjects compared to control women when faced with self-images; responses to other-images were similar. This suggests a potential variation in attention to or interpretation of self-images in AN. One might have expected a greater activation for AN subjects given their extreme sensitivity to their own appearance, however a conflation of self/other processing in AN patients might help maintain unrealistic ideas and expectations about their own bodies, and the unduly influence of appearances of others and media imagery [91]. Mohr [92] used size estimation to judge body dissatisfaction in AN women. It was found that AN women overestimated their own body size and reported greater satisfaction to images of underweight body types that most closely mirrored their ideal size. The insula and lateral prefrontal cortex showed increased activation to the underweight image as well, which was interpreted as a possible stronger emotional involvement, but could also be seen as a possible higher effort to estimate. In a study by Uher[93], using line drawings of underweight, normal, and overweight body sizes, along with a measurement of fear and disgust AN individuals rated the body images in all weight categories as more unpleasant than the control women. This study also found that the eating disordered individuals showed decreased activation in the lateral fusiform gyrus and the parietal cortex. Additionally, ratings of aversion were found to correlate with activation in the right medial apical prefrontal cortex. Another study [94] used an idealized body shape and asked participants to compare themselves to this body shape. It was found that the AN individuals demonstrated greater anxiety to the idealized body shape, versus the control, and hyperactivation of the insula and premotor cortex was seen, along with hypoactivation of the ACC. The authors of this study suggested that this may indicate the altered self-body comparison, or the motivation to an idealized body. Miyake [95] used morphed body images of participants in an fMRI study; AN-R, AN-BP, and control women showed amygdala activation in response to the overweight version of their image, whereas the prefrontal cortex was activated in the AN-BP and the control women, but not the AN-R women. A study of 18 control women ages 18-35 examined brain activation as women actively compared images of themselves to slim fashion models; this revealed activity in body shape-related areas including lateral fusiform gyri and right IPL, but also right lateral prefrontal and left ACC. Furthermore, activations in basal ganglia and amygdala were correlated with a self-report of anxiety generated by the task [94] strengthening the notion of involvement of those areas in anxiety modulation in AN. A study by Vocks[96] described the effects of cognitive behavioral body image therapy using fMRI. AN individuals were shown images of their own body before and after treatment with the cognitive behavioral body image therapy. It was found that the AN individuals after receiving this therapy had increased activation of the left middle temporal gyrus, including the extrastriate region and bilateral frontal regions including the middle frontal gyrus. These regions are important in the visual processing of self and treatment might improve attention to self. However, no control women were included in the study, making the relevance of the outcome in relation to the healthy state unclear.

Rather than image stimuli, a recent small study on mostly AN-B/P versus control women used words that were either neutral or associated with fatness or thinness in a Stroop task, in which subjects respond to a word stimulus according to the color the word is printed in rather than the word itself. In AN, it was found that there was a behavioral attention bias toward the fat/thin valence words, as well as unique activation patterns for each valence condition, with increases in left frontal and left insula-temporo-parietal junction activation with the thin valence, and decreases in left frontal and right parietal activation in the fat valence [97]. Notably absent was a variation in amygdala response, which might have been expected from other studies. However, amygdala activation was found in a recent study [98], which used negative body image words and neutral words. Here women with AN-R and AN-BP had increased amygdala activation in response to the negative body image words. In patients with AN-BP the left medial pre-frontal cortex was activated. The activation of the amygdala in response to the negative body image words suggested an increased fearfulness, which may be related to the strong fear of weight gain. The medial prefrontal cortex may suggest an attempt to regulate emotions associated with the body image words.

A developing area of AN imaging attempts to look directly at the neurophysiology of neuropsychological trait markers. Heightened anxious traits are well established in AN, and dopamine-mediated reward pathways have been implicated (see below). Wagner [99] used a monetary win/loss paradigm and found among recovered AN women a relationship between trait anxiety and response to wins and losses in the caudate. Furthermore, AN women had similar responses to positive and negative feedback in the anteroventral striatum, whereas controls' responses differed between positive and negative conditions. The overall striatal response was greater in the recovered AN women compared to controls. These findings suggest a variation in reward processing, and potentially a conflation between positive and negative stimuli that may help to explain AN individuals ability to effectively restrict food and maintain anhedonia. In a recent study by Castro-Fornieles[100], it was shown that AN individuals had increased activation of the temporal and parietal regions compared to controls in performing a working memory task; this difference, however, was found to resolve with recovery on follow up. Another study [101] showed that patients with subtypes of AN demonstrated different regional activation in performing a go no-go task. The AN-BP individuals showed increased activation of bilateral precentralgyri, anterior cingulate cortex, middle and superior temporal gyri, and in the hypothalamus and right dorsal prefrontal cortex. This suggests that there may be differing mechanisms with regard to impulse control between subtypes of eating disorders. In a study [102] using a task that tested how well subjects learned new rules or switched behavior responses, AN women were found to have hypoactivation of the anterior cingulate cortex, the thalamus, ventral striatum, sensorimotor brain regions, and cerebellum compared to control women and this brain response was associated with greater difficulties to switch behavior routines. There was also hyperactivation of the frontal and parietal regions that may suggest greater exertion in performing the task, while AN individuals had normal cognitive flexibility.

It is difficult to compare these studies as the imaging modalities and tasks are not consistent and the groups of subjects are small. Still, it appears that cingulate and prefrontal activity is frequently different between AN and control women. Those regions may be over-activated when confronted with anxiety-provoking food related stimuli. Such a heightened vigilance is probably related to anxious body and fear-of-fatness cognitions, followed by actions in order to avoid weight gain. On the other hand, AN subjects may respond less to expected taste and other reward stimuli, which may help to be able to restrict food intake, especially neurobiologically "rewarding" foods, but could be hypersensitive to salient stimuli and this could drive harm avoidance [84]. The results from the other imaging studies are not conclusive. However, it appears that AN do have altered self-perception related brain activation and this may suggest incorrect processing of, and maybe abnormal feedback from the body periphery, which in turn may allow over-valued ideas of thinness to control the self-image.

Receptor Imaging Studies

Neurotransmitters such as serotonin (5HT) or dopamine (DA) are distributed throughout the brain via specific neuronal pathways. Their influence on behavior is believed to be via action on specific receptors in, for example, the midbrain, the basal ganglia and neocortex. Radioligands exist for several of the 5HT receptor types. One of the most commonly assessed receptor types is the 5HT2A receptor, which is involved in the regulation of feeding, mood, and anxiety, and in antidepressant action [103]. Four studies have assessed 5HT2A receptor binding in ill and recovered AN women. Ill subjects showed reduced binding in the left frontal, bilateral parietal and occipital cortex [104]. Recovered AN-R also had reduced 5HT2A binding, most strongly in mesial temporal and parietal cortical areas as well as in the cingulate cortex [105]. In another study, women recovered from AN-B/P had reduced 5HT2A binding relative to controls in the left subgenual cingulate, left parietal, and right occipital cortex [106]. In that study 5HT2A binding was positively related to harm avoidance and negatively to novelty seeking in cingulate and temporal regions, with negative relationships between 5HT2A binding and drive for thinness. A later study by the same group [49] found normal 5HT2A binding in ill AN but replicated the correlation between 5HT2A activity and harm avoidance.

The 5HT2A findings further highlight the possibility of disturbances of the ACC and mesial temporal cortex in AN. Since these disturbances persist after recovery, it is possible they are trait disturbances. The ACC receives afferents from the amygdala and has direct projections to the premotor frontal cortex and other limbic regions. It plays a crucial role in initiation of and motivation for goal-directed behaviors [107] as well as computation of the future value of potentially rewarding stimuli [108]. In turn, the amygdala mediate the interpretation of fear and the representation of emotional stimuli values [74]. One could hypothesize that AN have disturbed processing of the valence of stimuli, resulting in poor flexibility in reevaluating actual danger of those stimuli together with reduced adaptation to new situations. This could lead to altered reward prediction and reduced drive to approach food rewards. Future studies will need to determine whether relationships between 5HT2A receptor activity and measures for anxiety such as harm avoidance can be replicated and expanded upon.

Another major serotonin receptor type is the 5HT1A receptor. The Bailer study mentioned above [40], as well as an earlier study from the same group [109], both examined 5HT1A, which is found throughout the forebrain as well as in the midbrain raphe nuclei. The 2005 study [109] of recovered AN-R, recovered AN-B/P, and recovered bulimic individuals found an increase in 5HT1A availability in the dorsal raphe and throughout the cortex in the AN-B/P and bulimic groups, but not in the AN-R group, raising the possibility of alternate pathogenetic pathways for binging/purging versus restricting behavior. The group's 2007 study [40] in ill AN-R and AN-BP, however, found increased 5HT1A activity in similar regions in both subtypes of AN, complicating the issue of this receptor's potential role in pathogenesis of the disease. Most recently, Galusca[110] examined 5HT1A binding in ill and recovered AN-R, finding similar profiles in both ill and recovered individuals of increased binding potential in frontal, temporal, parietal, and amygdala regions. The consistency of diffuse increase in 5HT1A receptor activity across these studies and levels of recovery suggests a potential trait disturbance in the serotonergic system.

Another study examined the serotonin transporter (5HT-T) activity among recovered AN-R and AN-B/P [111]. Each group revealed a distinct pattern of activity of this transporter in dorsal raphe and anteroventral striatum, with AN-

R > AN-B/P (neocortical binding could not be assessed due to a lack of specificity of the radioligand). This finding suggests one possible explanation for the variability in the affective traits associated with the different eating disorder subtypes; however subgroups have been small and replication is needed.

Only one study has so far examined dopamine receptor (D2/D3) activity in AN. Frank [112] found increased dopamine activity in the anteroventral striatum among recovered AN. This finding suggests an up-regulation of dopamine receptors, which may correspond to a prior finding of decreased CSF concentrations of dopamine metabolite in AN [113]. Specifically, high dopamine D2 receptor binding together with low brain dopamine [113] could be related to an inflexible dopamine system and low motivation in AN to approach stimuli that most people would find rewarding, including food [114]. Dopamine is implicated in the reward and addiction system, with decreased dopamine receptor activity associated with both addiction and obesity [115]. As such, the inverse finding in AN may help to account for both food restriction as well as the anhedonic and avoidant drive frequently seen in AN. Furthermore, a study by Bailer [116] that tested brain response to amphetamine induced dopamine release using PET showed that dopamine release was related to heightened anxiety in recovered AN. Thus, altered dopamine function could be difficult to normalize due to the high anxiety the AN Individuals have to overcome.

CONCLUSION

Until recently, the assessment of psychiatric disorders has relied on subjective reports from patients, and biologic research has been limited by the inaccessibility of the living human brain. The emergence of brain imaging techniques enables us to assess brain function *in vivo* and assess human behavior in conjunction with biological correlates. The new imaging methods give hope to the prospect of identifying biologic markers that will help conceptualize AN better from a biologic level and, in turn, identify more effective treatments that could reduce morbidity associated with this frequently debilitating and deadly illness.

Studying eating disorders is complicated due to a relatively small prevalence and the many state-related (e.g. hormonal, nutritional) disturbances associated with these illnesses. Thus, it is difficult to assess factors that may be trait related and possibly pre-morbid. Studying subjects after long-term recovery may be our closest approximation to studying subjects premorbidly.

That approach, however, carries uncertainty as to whether the results obtained are truly pre-morbid conditions, or represent a "scar" from the illness. Ideally, studies during the ill state correct for state dependent confounds (such as partial volume correction for reversible brain reductions) but test disorder-specific behaviors in relation to specific functional brain abnormalities.

The common global reductions of grey and white matter in ill AN remit at least in part with recovery. It is possible that the explanation for reduction in brain mass when ill may be brain protein, fat, or fluid loss secondary to emaciation and dehydration. However, since some eating disorder studies but not others found relationships of brain volume with cortisol levels as well as cortisol related to brain cell death [117] it remains to be assessed whether hypercortisolemia in ill AN is truly contributing to those findings.

Resting rCBF and rCGM in AN and bulimiashowed mostly a general reduced cortical activity in the ill state that is most pronounced in temporal, parietal or cingulate cortex. Very limited data suggest some persistence of these findings after recovery in AN, though recent research in recovered subjects disagreed and did not suggest that rCBF/cCGM studies should be made a main focus of future research.

Functional MRI studies using visual stimuli of food or body image in AN have had variegated approaches and outcomes. Broadly, their results have most often implicated involvement of prefrontal, ACC, temporal and parietal cortices, with exaggerated brain response to anxiety-provoking food stimuli. In contrast, readily distinguishable taste stimuli indicate a general reduction of brain response in recovered AN. Whether reduced brain response to otherwise rewarding stimuli is cognitively or more biologically driven will be an important next step in AN research.

The neurotransmitter receptor imaging studies that are available at this point in AN show that increased 5HT1A receptor binding occurs in the ill state, while 5HT2A binding appears normal. After recovery, AN-R and AN-BP have reduced 5HT2A binding, while 5HT1A availability is elevated in AN-BP and possibly elevated in AN-R. Such findings of 5HT disturbances in ill and recovered subjects with eating disorders, strongly suggests a trait disturbance of the 5HT system. Altered 5HT receptor activity could be related to emotional disturbances such as increased depressive symptoms or anxiety. However, the exact mechanisms of neuroreceptor-behavior interactions needs further study.

Few studies have been done in eating disorders in comparison to depressive disorders or obsessive compulsive disorder. The overlap and comorbidity of both major depression and obsessive compulsive disorder with eating disorders require studies that will directly compare those disorders. Eating disorders, in particular AN, are frequently debilitating with a high mortality. Studies comparing psychiatric disorders will help to find common pathways and distinct areas of disturbance that may identify targets for successful drug interventions.

Lastly, the combination of various imaging techniques such as fMRI and ERP may hold the promise of relating real time neuronal activity with behavior and good spatial localization. New techniques will enable new types of imaging studies in eating disorders, for example, manganese-enhanced MRI (MEMRI), which uses manganese ion as a blood flow-related contrast medium, was recently used to track binding of the appetite-stimulating gut hormone ghrelin and the appetite-suppressing peptide $YY_{3\text{-}36}$ in mouse brains, allowing for examination of the time course of hormone binding in the hypothalamus versus appetitive behavior [118]. Tracking the brain-hormone link in humans will unfold a new wrinkle in the evolving study of eating disorders.

Taken together, the last few decades have shown significant advances in the study of eating disorder neurobiology, but the specific relationships between eating disorder traits and behaviors and brain function remain obscure. This will be the task of the next generation of brain imaging studies in eating disorders.

References

[1] Task Force on DSM-IV, A. P. A. *Diagnostic and Statistical Manual of Mental Disorders DSM-IV-TR (Text Revision).* Washington, DC. USA.: American Psychiatric Press; 1994.

[2] Bulik CM, Sullivan PF, Fear JL, PR., J. (1997). Eating disorders and antecedent anxiety disorders: a controlled study. *Acta Psychiatr Scand, 96*, 101-7.

[3] Ohman, A., Carlsson, K., Lundqvist, D., Ingvar, M. (2007). On the unconscious subcortical origin of human fear. *Physiol Behav, 92*, 180-5.

[4] Konarski, J. Z., McIntyre, R. S., Soczynska, J. K., Kennedy, S. H. (2007). Neuroimaging approaches in mood disorders: technique and clinical implications. *Ann Clin Psychiatry, 19*, 265-77.

[5] Chau, D. T., Roth, R. M., Green, A. I. (2004). The neural circuitry of reward and its relevance to psychiatric disorders. *Curr Psychiatry Rep, 6*, 391-9.

[6] Alvarez, J. A., Emory, E. (2006). Executive Function and the Frontal Lobes: A Meta-Analytic Review. *Neuropsychol Rev*, 16, 17-42.

[7] Hentschel, F., Besthorn, C., Schmidt, M. H. (1997). Die fraktale Dimension als Bildbearbeitungsparameter im CT bei Anorexia nervosa vor und nach Therapie. *Zeitschrift fur Kinder-und Jugendpsychiatrie und Psychotherapie*, *25*, 201-6.

[8] Hentschel, F., Schmidbauer, M., Detzner, U., Blanz, B., Schmidt, M. H. (1995). Reversible Hirnvolumenanderungen bei der Anorexia nervosa. *Zeitschrift fur Kinder- und Jugendpsychiatrie*, *23*, 104-12.

[9] Kornreich, L., Shapira, A., Horev, G., Danziger, Y., Tyano, S., Mimouni, M. (1991). CT and MR evaluation of the brain in patients with anorexia nervosa. *American Journal of Neuroradiology*, *12*, 1213-6.

[10] Golden, NH., Ashtari, M., Kohn, M., Patel, M., Jacobson, M., Fletcher, A., Shenker, I. (1996). Reversibility of cerebral ventricular enlargement in anorexia nervosa, demonstrated by quantitative magnetic resonance imaging. *J Pediatr*, *128*, 296-301.

[11] Swayze, V. n., Andersen, A., Arndt, S., Rajarethinam, R., Fleming, F., Sato, Y., Andreasen, N. (1996). Reversibility of brain tissue loss in anorexia nervosa assessed with a computerized Talairach 3-D proportional grid. *Psychol Med*, *26*, 381-90.

[12] Katzman, D. K., Colangelo, J. J. (1996). Cerebral gray matter and white matter volume deficits in adolescent girls with anorexia nervosa.[comment]. *Health Law in Canada*, *16*, 110-4.

[13] Husain, M. M., Black, K. J., Doraiswamy, P. M., Shah, S. A., Rockwell, W. J., Ellinwood, E. H., Jr., Krishnan, K. R. (1992). Subcortical brain anatomy in anorexia and bulimia. *Biological Psychiatry*, *31*, 735-8.

[14] Lambe EK, Katzman DK, Mikulis DJ, Kennedy SH, RB., Z. (1997). Cerebral gray matter volume deficits after weight recovery from anorexia nervosa. *Arch Gen Psychiatry*, *54*, 537-42.

[15] Katzman, D. K., Kaptein, S., Kirsh, C., Brewer, H., Kalmbach, K., Olmsted, M. P., Woodside, D. B., Kaplan, A. S. (1997). A longitudinal magnetic resonance imaging study of brain changes in adolescents with anorexia nervosa. *Comprehensive Psychiatry*, *38*, 321-6.

[16] Muhlau, M., Gaser, C., Ilg, R., Conrad, B., Leibl, C., Cebulla, M. H., Backmund, H., Gerlinghoff, M., Lommer, P., Schnebel, A., Wohlschlager, A. M., Zimmer, C., Nunnemann, S. (2007). Gray matter decrease of the anterior cingulate cortex in anorexia nervosa. *Am J Psychiatry*, *164*, 1850-7.

[17] McCormick, L. M., Keel, P. K., Brumm, M. C., Bowers, W., Swayze, V., Andersen, A., Andreasen, N. (2008). Implications of starvation-induced change in right dorsal anterior cingulate volume in anorexia nervosa. *Int J Eat Disord*, *41*, 602-10.

[18] Wagner, A., Greer, P., Bailer, U. F., Frank, G. K., Henry, S. E., Putnam, K., Meltzer, C. C., Ziolko, S. K., Hoge, J., McConaha, C., Kaye, W. H. (2006). Normal brain tissue volumes after long-term recovery in anorexia and bulimia nervosa. *Biol Psychiatry*, *59*, 291-3.

[19] Castro-Fornieles, J., Bargallo, N., Lazaro, L., Andres, S., Falcon, C., Plana, M. T., Junque, C. (2009). A cross-sectional and follow-up voxel-based morphometric MRI study in adolescent anorexia nervosa. *J Psychiatr Res*, *43*, 331-40.

[20] Roberto, C. A., Mayer, L. E., Brickman, A. M., Barnes, A., Muraskin, J., Yeung, L. K., Steffener, J., Sy, M., Hirsch, J., Stern, Y., Walsh, B. T. (2011). Brain tissue volume changes following weight gain in adults with anorexia nervosa. *The International journal of eating disorders*, *44*, 406-11.

[21] Gwirtsman, H., Kaye, W., George, D., Jimerson, D., Ebert, M., Gold, P. (1989). Central and peripheral ACTH and cortisol levels in anorexia nervosa and bulimia. *Arch Gen Psychiatry*, *46*, 61-9.

[22] Ganong, W. *Review of Medical Physiology.* 22nd ed. New York: The

[23] Giordano, G., Renzetti, P., Parodi, R., Foppiani, L., Zandrino, F., Sardanelli, F. (2001). Volume measurement with magnetic resonance imaging of hippocampus-amygdala formation in patients with anorexia nervosa. *J Endocrinol Invest*, *24*, 510-4.

[24] Kingston, K., Szmukler, G., Andrewes, D., Tress, B., Desmond, P. (1996). Neuropsychological and structural brain changes in anorexia nervosa before and after refeeding. *Psychol Med*, *26*, 15-28.

[25] Connan, F., Murphy, F., Connor, S. E., Rich, P., Murphy, T., Bara-Carill, N., Landau, S., Krljes, S., Ng, V., Williams, S., Morris, R. G., Campbell, I. C., Treasure, J. (2006). Hippocampal volume and cognitive function in anorexia nervosa. *Psychiatry Res*, *146*, 117-25.

[26] Kazlouski, D., Rollin, M. D., Tregellas, J., Shott, M. E., Jappe, L. M., Hagman, J. O., Pryor, T., Yang, T. T., Frank, G. K. (2011). Altered fimbria-fornix white matter integrity in anorexia nervosa predicts harm avoidance. *Psychiatry research*, *192*, 109-16.

[27] Hentschel, J., Mockel, R., Schlemmer, H. P., Markus, A., Gopel, C., Guckel, F., Kopke, J., Georgi, M., Schmidt, M. H. (1999). 1H-MR-Spektroskopie bei Anorexia nervosa: charakteristische Unterschiede

zwischen Patienten und gesunden Probanden. *ROFO-Fortschritte auf dem Gebiet der Rontgenstrahlen und der Bildgebenden V*, *170*, 284-9.

[28] Schlemmer, H. P., Mockel, R., Marcus, A., Hentschel, F., Gopel, C., Becker, G., Kopke, J., Guckel, F., Schmidt, M. H., Georgi, M. (1998). Proton magnetic resonance spectroscopy in acute, juvenile anorexia nervosa. *Psychiatry Research*, *82*, 171-9.

[29] Mockel, R., Schlemmer, H. P., Guckel, F., Gopel, C., Becker, G., Kopke, J., Hentschel, F., Schmidt, M., Georgi, M. (1999). 1H-MR-Spektroskopie bei Anorexia nervosa: reversible zerebrale Metabolitenanderungen. *ROFO-Fortschritte auf dem Gebiet der Rontgenstrahlen und der Bildgebenden V*, *170*, 371-7.

[30] Roser, W., Bubl, R., Buergin, D., Seelig, J., Radue, E. W., Rost, B. (1999). Metabolic changes in the brain of patients with anorexia and bulimia nervosa as detected by proton magnetic resonance spectroscopy. *Int J Eat Disord*, *26*, 119-36.

[31] Rzanny, R., Freesmeyer, D., Reichenbach, J. R., Mentzel, H. J., Pfleiderer, S. O., Klemm, S., Gerhard, U. J., Blanz, B., Kaiser, W. A. (2003). 31P-MRS des Hirns bei Anorexia nervosa: Charakteristische Unterschiede in den Spektren von Patienten und gesunden Vergleichspersonen. *ROFO-Fortschritte auf dem Gebiet der Rontgenstrahlen und der Bildgebenden V*, *175*, 75-82.

[32] Leonard, B. E. (1994). Serotonin receptors--where are they going? *International Clinical Psychopharmacology*, *9 Suppl 1*, 7-17.

[33] Kaye, W. H., Klump, K. L., Frank, G. K., Strober, M. (2000). Anorexia and bulimia nervosa. *Annu Rev Med*, *51*, 299-313.

[34] Joos, A. A., Perlov, E., Buchert, M., Hartmann, A., Saum, B., Glauche, V., Freyer, T., Weber-Fahr, W., Zeeck, A., Tebartz van Elst, L. (2011). Magnetic resonance spectroscopy of the anterior cingulate cortex in eating disorders. *Psychiatry research*, *191*, 196-200.

[35] Gordon, I., Lask, B., Bryant-Waugh, R., Christie, D., Timimi, S. (1997). Childhood-onset anorexia nervosa: towards identifying a biological substrate. *Int J Eat Disord*, *22*, 159-65.

[36] Kuruoglu, A. C., Kapucu, O., Atasever, T., Arikan, Z., Isik, E., Unlu, M. (1998). Technetium-99m-HMPAO brain SPECT in anorexia nervosa. *J Nucl Med*, *39*, 304-6.

[37] Takano, A., Shiga, T., Kitagawa, N., Koyama, T., Katoh, C., Tsukamoto, E., Tamaki, N. (2001). Abnormal neuronal network in anorexia nervosa studied with I-123-IMP SPECT. *Psychiatry Research: Neuroimaging*, *107(1) Jul 2001*, 45-50.

[38] Chowdhury U, Gordon I, Lask B, Watkins B, Watt H, D., C. (2003). Early-onset anorexia nervosa: is there evidence of limbic system imbalance? *International Journal of Eating Disorders*, *33*, 388-96.

[39] Rastam, M., Bjure, J., Vestergren, E., Uvebrant, P., Gillberg, I. C., Wentz, E., Gillberg, C. (2001). Regional cerebral blood flow in weight-restored anorexia nervosa: a preliminary study. *Dev Med Child Neurol*, *43*, 239-42.

[40] Bailer, U. F., Frank, G. K., Henry, S. E., Price, J. C., Meltzer, C. C., Mathis, C. A., Wagner, A., Thornton, L., Hoge, J., Ziolko, S. K., Becker, C. R., McConaha, C. W., Kaye, W. H. (2007). Exaggerated 5-HT1A but Normal 5-HT2A Receptor Activity in Individuals Ill with Anorexia Nervosa. *Biol Psychiatry*, 61,1090-99.

[41] Kojima, S., Nagai, N., Nakabeppu, Y., Muranaga, T., Deguchi, D., Nakajo, M., Masuda, A., Nozoe, S., Naruo, T. (2005). Comparison of regional cerebral blood flow in patients with anorexia nervosa before and after weight gain. *Psychiatry Res*, *140*, 251-8.

[42] Matsumoto, R., Kitabayashi, Y., Narumoto, J., Wada, Y., Okamoto, A., Ushijima, Y., Yokoyama, C., Yamashita, T., Takahashi, H., Yasuno, F., Suhara, T., Fukui, K. (2006). Regional cerebral blood flow changes associated with interoceptive awareness in the recovery process of anorexia nervosa. *Prog Neuropsychopharmacol Biol Psychiatry*, 30, 1265-70.

[43] Bruch, H. (1962). Perceptual and conceptual disturbances in anorexia nervosa. *Psychosom Med*, *24*, 187-94.

[44] Frank, G. K., Bailer, U. F., Meltzer, C. C., Price, J. C., Mathis, C. A., Wagner, A., Becker, C., Kaye, W. H., Frank, G. K., Bailer, U. F., Meltzer, C. C., Price, J. C., Mathis, C. A., Wagner, A., Becker, C., Kaye, W. H. (2007). Regional cerebral blood flow after recovery from anorexia or bulimia nervosa. *International Journal of Eating Disorders*, *40*, 488-92.

[45] Delvenne, V., Goldman, S., Biver, F., De Maertalaer, V., Wikler, D., Damhaut, P., Lotstra, F. (1997). Brain hypometabolism of glucose in low-weight depressed patients and in anorectic patients: a consequence of starvation? *Journalof Affective Disorders*, *44*, 69-77.

[46] Delvenne, V., Goldman, S., De Maertelaer, V., Wikler, D., Damhaut, P., Lotstra, F. (1997). Brain glucose metabolism in anorexia nervosa and affective disorders: influence of weight loss or depressive symptomatology. *Psychiatry Research: Neuroimaging*, *74*, 83-92.

[47] Delvenne, V., Goldman, S., DeMaertelaer, V., Simon, Y., Luxen, A., Lotstra, F. (1996). Brain hypometabolism of glucose in anorexia nervosa: normalization after weight gain. *Biol Psychiatry*, *40*, 761-8.

[48] Delvenne, V., Lotstra, F., Goldman, S., Biver, F., De, M., V, Appelboom-Fondu, J., Schoutens, A., Bidaut, L. M., Luxen, A., Mendelwicz, J. (1995). Brain hypometabolism of glucose in anorexia nervosa: a PET scan study. *Biological Psychiatry*, *37*, 161-9.

[49] Bailer, U. F., Frank, G. K., Henry, S. E., Price, J. C., Meltzer, C. C., Mathis, C. A., Wagner, A., Thornton, L., Hoge, J., Ziolko, S. K., Becker, C. R., McConaha, C. W., Kaye, W. H., Bailer, U. F., Frank, G. K., Henry, S. E., Price, J. C., Meltzer, C. C., Mathis, C. A., Wagner, A., Thornton, L., Hoge, J., Ziolko, S. K., Becker, C. R., McConaha, C. W., Kaye, W. H. (2007). Exaggerated 5-HT1A but normal 5-HT2A receptor activity in individuals ill with anorexia nervosa. *Biological Psychiatry*, *61*, 1090-9.

[50] Frank, G. K., Bailer, U. F., Meltzer, C. C., Price, J. C., Mathis, C. A., Wagner, A., Becker, C., Kaye, W. H. (2007). Regional cerebral blood flow after recovery from anorexia or bulimia nervosa. *Int J Eat Disord*, *40*, 488-92.

[51] Yonezawa, H., Otagaki, Y., Miyake, Y., Okamoto, Y., Yamawaki, S. (2008). No differences are seen in the regional cerebral blood flow in the restricting type of anorexia nervosa compared with the binge eating/purging type. *Psychiatry Clin Neurosci*, *62*, 26-33.

[52] Goethals, I., Vervaet, M., Audenaert, K., Jacobs, F., Ham, H., Van de Wiele, C., Vandecapelle, M., Slegers, G., Dierckx, R., van Heeringen, C. (2007). Differences of cortical 5-HT(2A) receptor binding index with SPECT in subtypes of anorexia nervosa: Relationship with personality traits? *J Psychiatr Res*, *41*, 455-8.

[53] Martin, F. (1955). [Pathological neurological and psychiatric aspects of some deficiency manifestations with digestive and neuro-endocrine disorders. II. Studies of the changes in the central nervous system in two cases of anorexia (so-called anorexia nervosa) in young girls.]. *Helv Med Acta*, *22*, 522-9.

[54] Crisp, A. H., Fenton, G. W., Scotton, L. (1967). The electroencephalogram in anorexia nervosa. *Electroencephalogr Clin Neurophysiol*, *23*, 490.

[55] Lacey, J. H., Crisp, A. H., Kalucy, R. S., Hartmann, M. K., Chien, C. N. (1975). Weight gain and the sleeping electroencephalogram: study of 10 patients with anorexia nervosa. *Br Med J*, *4*, 556-8.

[56] Bradley, S. J., Taylor, M. J., Rovet, J. F., Goldberg, E., Hood, J., Wachsmuth, R., Azcue, M. P., Pencharz, P. B. (1997). Assessment of brain function in adolescent anorexia nervosa before and after weight gain. *J Clin Exp Neuropsychol*, *19*, 20-33.

[57] Dodin, V., Nandrino, J. L. (2003). Cognitive processing of anorexic patients in recognition tasks: an event-related potentials study. *Int J Eat Disord*, *33*, 299-307.

[58] Pieters, G. L., de Bruijn, E. R., Maas, Y., Hulstijn, W., Vandereycken, W., Peuskens, J., Sabbe, B. G. (2007). Action monitoring and perfectionism in anorexia nervosa. *Brain Cogn*, *63*, 42-50.

[59] Kaye, W., Bastiani, A., Moss, H. (1995). Cognitive style of patients with anorexia nervosa and bulimia nervosa. *International Journal of Eating Disorders*, *18*, 287-90.

[60] Carter, C. S., Braver, T. S., Barch, D. M., Botvinick, M. M., Noll, D., Cohen, J. D. (1998). Anterior cingulate cortex, error detection, and the online monitoring of performance. *Science*, *280*, 747-9.

[61] Kiehl, K. A., Liddle, P. F., Hopfinger, J. B. (2000). Error processing and the rostral anterior cingulate: an event-related fMRI study. *Psychophysiology*, *37*, 216-23.

[62] Pollatos, O., Herbert, B. M., Schandry, R., Gramann, K. (2008). Impaired central processing of emotional faces in anorexia nervosa. *Psychosom Med*, *70*, 701-8.

[63] Grunwald, M., Weiss, T., Assmann, B., Ettrich, C., Grunwald, M., Weiss, T., Assmann, B., Ettrich, C. (2004). Stable asymmetric interhemispheric theta power in patients with anorexia nervosa during haptic perception even after weight gain: a longitudinal study. *Journal of Clinical & Experimental Neuropsychology: Official Journal of the International Neuropsychological Society*, *26*, 608-20.

[64] Klem, G. H., Luders, H. O., Jasper, H. H., Elger, C. (1999). The ten-twenty electrode system of the International Federation. The International Federation of Clinical Neurophysiology. *Electro-encephalogr Clin Neurophysiol Suppl*, *52*, 3-6.

[65] Rodriguez, G., Babiloni, C., Brugnolo, A., Del Percio, C., Cerro, F., Gabrielli, F., Girtler, N., Nobili, F., Murialdo, G., Rossini, P. M., Rossi, D. S., Baruzzi, C., Ferro, A. M., Rodriguez, G., Babiloni, C., Brugnolo, A., Del Percio, C., Cerro, F., Gabrielli, F., Girtler, N., Nobili, F., Murialdo, G., Rossini, P. M., Rossi, D. S., Baruzzi, C., Ferro, A. M. (2007). Cortical sources of awake scalp EEG in eating disorders. *Clin Neurophysiol*, *118*, 1213-22.

[66] Besthorn, C., Zerfass, R., Geiger-Kabisch, C., Sattel, H., Daniel, S., Schreiter-Gasser, U., Forstl, H. (1997). Discrimination of Alzheimer's disease and normal aging by EEG data. *Electroencephalogr Clin Neurophysiol*, *103*, 241-8.

[67] Jelic, V., Shigeta, M., Julin, P., Almkvist, O., Winblad, B., Wahlund, L. O. (1996). Quantitative electroencephalography power and coherence in Alzheimer's disease and mild cognitive impairment. *Dementia*, *7*, 314-23.

[68] Moretti, D. V., Babiloni, C., Binetti, G., Cassetta, E., Dal Forno, G., Ferreric, F., Ferri, R., Lanuzza, B., Miniussi, C., Nobili, F., Rodriguez, G., Salinari, S., Rossini, P. M. (2004). Individual analysis of EEG frequency and band power in mild Alzheimer's disease. *Clin Neurophysiol*, *115*, 299-308.

[69] Nozoe, S., Naruo, T., Nakabeppu, Y., Soejima, Y., Nakajo, M., Tanaka, H. (1993). Changes in regional cerebral blood flow in patients with anorexia nervosa detected through single photon emission tomography imaging. *Biol Psychiatry*, *34*, 578-80.

[70] Nozoe, S., Naruo, T., Yonekura, R., Nakabeppu, Y., Soejima, Y., Nagai, N., Nakajo, M., Tanaka, H. (1995). Comparison of regional cerebral blood flow in patients with eating disorders. *Brain Res Bull*, *36*, 251-5.

[71] Naruo, T., Nakabeppu, Y., Sagiyama, K., Munemoto, T., Homan, N., Deguchi, D., Nakajo, M., Nozoe, S. (2000). Characteristic regional cerebral blood flow patterns in anorexia nervosa patients with binge/purge behavior. *Am J Psychiatry*, *157*, 1520-2.

[72] Gordon, C., Dougherty, D., Fischman, A., Emans, S., Grace, E., Lamm, R., Alpert, N., Majzoub, J., Rauch, S. (2001). Neural substrates of anorexia nervosa: a behavioral challenge study with positron emission tomography. *J Pediatr*, *139*, 51-7.

[73] Ellison, A. R., Fong, J. Neuroimaging in Eating Disorders. In: Hoek H. W., Treasure J. L., Katzman M. A., editors. *Neurobiology in the treatment of eating disorders*. Chichester: John Wiley & Sons LTd.; 1998. p. 255-69.

[74] LeDoux, J. (2003). The emotional brain, fear, and the amygdala. *Cell Mol Neurobiol*, *23*, 727-38.

[75] Uher R, Brammer MJ, Murphy T, Campbell IC, Ng VW, Williams SC, J., T. (2003). Recovery and chronicity in anorexia nervosa: brain activity associated with differential outcomes. *Biol Psychiatry*, *54*, 934-42.

[76] Joos, A. A., Saum, B., van Elst, L. T., Perlov, E., Glauche, V., Hartmann, A., Freyer, T., Tuscher, O., Zeeck, A. (2011). Amygdala

hyperreactivity in restrictive anorexia nervosa. *Psychiatry research*, *191*, 189-95.

[77] Santel, S., Baving, L., Krauel, K., Munte, T. F., Rotte, M. (2006). Hunger and satiety in anorexia nervosa: fMRI during cognitive processing of food pictures. *Brain Res*, *1114*, 138-48.

[78] Gizewski, E. R., Rosenberger, C., de Greiff, A., Moll, A., Senf, W., Wanke, I., Forsting, M., Herpertz, S. (2010). Influence of satiety and subjective valence rating on cerebral activation patterns in response to visual stimulation with high-calorie stimuli among restrictive anorectic and control women. *Neuropsychobiology*, *62*, 182-92.

[79] Wagner, A., Aizenstein, H., Mazurkewicz, L., Fudge, J., Frank, G. K., Putnam, K., Bailer, U. F., Fischer, L., Kaye, W. H. (2008). Altered insula response to taste stimuli in individuals recovered from restricting-type anorexia nervosa. *Neuropsychopharmacology : official publication of the American College of Neuropsychopharmacology*, *33*, 513-23.

[80] Craig, A. D. (2002). How do you feel? Interoception: the sense of the physiological condition of the body. *Nat Rev Neurosci*, *3*, 655-66.

[81] Bush, G., Vogt, B. A., Holmes, J., Dale, A. M., Greve, D., Jenike, M. A., Rosen, B. R. (2002). Dorsal anterior cingulate cortex: A role in reward-based decision making. *Proc Natl Acad Sci USA*, *99*, 523-8.

[82] Vocks, S., Herpertz, S., Rosenberger, C., Senf, W., Gizewski, E. R. (2011). Effects of gustatory stimulation on brain activity during hunger and satiety in females with restricting-type anorexia nervosa: an fMRI study. *Journal of psychiatric research*, *45*, 395-403.

[83] Cowdrey, F. A., Park, R. J., Harmer, C. J., McCabe, C. (2011). Increased Neural Processing of Rewarding and Aversive Food Stimuli in Recovered Anorexia Nervosa. *Biological Psychiatry*.

[84] Jappe, L. M., Frank, G. K., Shott, M. E., Rollin, M. D., Pryor, T., Hagman, J. O., Yang, T. T., Davis, E. (2011). Heightened sensitivity to reward and punishment in anorexia nervosa. *Int J Eat Disord*, *44*, 317-24.

[85] Seeger G, Braus DF, Ruf M, Goldberger U, MH., S. (2002). Body image distortion reveals amygdala activation in patients with anorexia nervosa -- a functional magnetic resonance imaging study. *Neurosci Lett*, *326*, 25-8.

[86] Wagner A, Ruf M, Braus DF, MH., S. (2003). Neuronal activity changes and body image distortion in anorexia nervosa. *Neuroreport*, *14*, 2193-7.

[87] Giummarra, M. J., Gibson, S. J., Georgiou-Karistianis, N., Bradshaw, J. L. (2008). Mechanisms underlying embodiment, disembodiment and loss of embodiment. *Neurosci Biobehav Rev*, *32*, 143-60.

[88] Shirao N, Okamoto Y, Okada G, Okamoto Y, S., Y. (2003). Temporomesial activation in young females associated with unpleasant words concerning body image. *Neuropsychobiology*, *48*, 136-42.

[89] Fladung, A. K., Gron, G., Grammer, K., Herrnberger, B., Schilly, E., Grasteit, S., Wolf, R. C., Walter, H., von Wietersheim, J. (2010). A neural signature of anorexia nervosa in the ventral striatal reward system. *Am J Psychiatry*, *167*, 206-12.

[90] Sachdev, P., Mondraty, N., Wen, W., Gulliford, K. (2008). Brains of anorexia nervosa patients process self-images differently from non-self-images: an fMRI study. *Neuropsychologia*, *46*, 2161-8.

[91] Borzekowski, D. L., Robinson, T. N. (2005). The remote, the mouse, and the no. 2 pencil: the household media environment and academic achievement among third grade students. *Arch Pediatr Adolesc Med*, *159*, 607-13.

[92] Mohr, H. M., Zimmermann, J., Roder, C., Lenz, C., Overbeck, G., Grabhorn, R. (2010). Separating two components of body image in anorexia nervosa using fMRI. *Psychological medicine*, *40*, 1519-29.

[93] Uher, R., Murphy, T., Friederich, H. C., Dalgleish, T., Brammer, M. J., Giampietro, V., Phillips, M. L., Andrew, C., Ng, V. W., Williams, C. R., Campbell, I. C., Treasure, J. (2005). Functional Neuroanatomy of Body Shape Perception in Healthy and eating-Disordered Women. *Biological Psychiatry*, *58*, 990-7.

[94] Friederich, H. C., Brooks, S., Uher, R., Campbell, I. C., Giampietro, V., Brammer, M., Williams, S. C., Herzog, W., Treasure, J. (2010). Neural correlates of body dissatisfaction in anorexia nervosa. *Neuropsychologia*, *48*, 2878-85.

[95] Miyake, Y., Okamoto, Y., Onoda, K., Kurosaki, M., Shirao, N., Yamawaki, S. (2010). Brain activation during the perception of distorted body images in eating disorders. *Psychiatry research*, *181*, 183-92.

[96] Vocks, S., Schulte, D., Busch, M., Gronemeyer, D., Herpertz, S., Suchan, B. (2011). Changes in neuronal correlates of body image processing by means of cognitive-behavioural body image therapy for eating disorders: a randomized controlled fMRI study. *Psychological medicine*, *41*, 1651-63.

[97] Redgrave, G. W., Bakker, A., Bello, N. T., Caffo, B. S., Coughlin, J. W., Guarda, A. S., McEntee, J. E., Pekar, J. J., Reinblatt, S. P., Verduzco, G.,

Moran, T. H. (2008). Differential brain activation in anorexia nervosa to Fat and Thin words during a Stroop task. *Neuroreport*, *19*, 1181-5.

[98] Miyake, Y., Okamoto, Y., Onoda, K., Shirao, N., Otagaki, Y., Yamawaki, S. (2010). Neural processing of negative word stimuli concerning body image in patients with eating disorders: an fMRI study. *Neuroimage*, *50*, 1333-9.

[99] Wagner, A., Aizenstein, H., Venkatraman, V. K., Fudge, J., May, J. C., Mazurkewicz, L., Frank, G. K., Bailer, U. F., Fischer, L., Nguyen, V., Carter, C., Putnam, K., Kaye, W. H. (2007). Altered reward processing in women recovered from anorexia nervosa. *Am J Psychiatry*, *164*, 1842-9.

[100] Castro-Fornieles, J., Bargallo, N., Lazaro, L., Andres, S., Falcon, C., Plana, M. T., Junque, C. (2009). A cross-sectional and follow-up voxel-based morphometric MRI study in adolescent anorexia nervosa. *J Psychiatr Res*, 43, 331-340.

[101] Lock, J., Garrett, A., Beenhakker, J., Reiss, A. L. (2011). Aberrant brain activation during a response inhibition task in adolescent eating disorder subtypes. *The American journal of psychiatry*, *168*, 55-64.

[102] Zastrow, A., Kaiser, S., Stippich, C., Walther, S., Herzog, W., Tchanturia, K., Belger, A., Weisbrod, M., Treasure, J., Friederich, H. C. (2009). Neural correlates of impaired cognitive-behavioral flexibility in anorexia nervosa. *Am J Psychiatry*, *166*, 608-16.

[103] Barnes, N. M., Sharp, T. (1999). A review of central 5-HT receptors and their function. *Neuropharmacology*, *38*, 1083-152.

[104] Audenaert K, Van Laere K, Dumont F, Vervaet M, Goethals I, Slegers G, Mertens J, van Heeringen C, RA., D. (2003). Decreased 5-HT2a receptor binding in patients with anorexia nervosa. *J Nucl Med*, *44*, 163-9.

[105] Frank, G., Kaye, W., Meltzer, C., Price, J., Greer, P., McConaha, C., K., S. (2002). Reduced 5-HT2A receptor binding after recovery from anorexia nervosa. *Biol Psychiatry*, *52*, 896-906.

[106] Bailer, U., Price JC, Meltzer CC, Mathis CA, Frank GK, Weissfeld L, McConaha CW, Henry SE, Brooks-Achenbach S, Barbarich NC, Walter H Kaye. (2004). Altered 5-HT2A Receptor Activity after Recovery from Bulimia-type Anorexia Nervosa: Relationships to Harm Avoidance and Drive for Thinness. *Neuropsychopharmacology*, *29*, 1143-55.

[107] Devinsky O, Morrell MJ, BA., V. (1995). Contributions of anterior cingulate cortex to behaviour. *Brain*, *118*, 279-306.

[108] Richmond, B., Liu, Z., Shidara, M. (2003). Neuroscience. Predicting future rewards. *Science*, *301*, 179-80.

[109] Bailer, U. F., Frank, G. K., Henry, S. E., Price, J. C., Meltzer, C. C., Weissfeld, L., Mathis, C. A., Drevets, W. C., Wagner, A., Hoge, J., Ziolko, S. K., McConaha, C. W., Kaye, W. H. (2005). Altered brain serotonin 5-HT1A receptor binding after recovery from anorexia nervosa measured by positron emission tomography and [carbonyl11C]WAY-100635. *Arch Gen Psychiatry*, *62*, 1032-41.

[110] Galusca, B., Costes, N., Zito, N. G., Peyron, R., Bossu, C., Lang, F., Le Bars, D., Estour, B. (2008). Organic background of restrictive-type anorexia nervosa suggested by increased serotonin 1A receptor binding in right frontotemporal cortex of both lean and recovered patients: [18F]MPPF PET scan study. *Biol Psychiatry*, *64*, 1009-13.

[111] Bailer, U. F., Frank, G. K., Henry, S. E., Price, J. C., Meltzer, C. C., Becker, C., Ziolko, S. K., Mathis, C. A., Wagner, A., Barbarich-Marsteller, N. C., Putnam, K., Kaye, W. H. (2007). Serotonin transporter binding after recovery from eating disorders. *Psychopharmacology (Berl)*, *195*, 315-24.

[112] Frank, G. K., Bailer, U. F., Henry, S. E., Drevets, W., Meltzer, C. C., Price, J. C., Mathis, C. A., Wagner, A., Hoge, J., Ziolko, S., Barbarich-Marsteller, N., Weissfeld, L., Kaye, W. H. (2005). Increased dopamine D2/D3 receptor binding after recovery from anorexia nervosa measured by positron emission tomography and [11c]raclopride. *Biol Psychiatry*, *58*, 908-12.

[113] Kaye, W. H., Ebert, M. H., Raleigh, M., Lake, R. (1984). Abnormalities in CNS monoamine metabolism in anorexia nervosa. *Arch Gen Psychiatry*, *41*, 350-5.

[114] Kelley, A. E., Berridge, K. C. (2002). The neuroscience of natural rewards: relevance to addictive drugs. *J Neurosci*, *22*, 3306-11.

[115] Wang, G. J., Volkow, N. D., Thanos, P. K., Fowler, J. S. (2004). Similarity between obesity and drug addiction as assessed by neurofunctional imaging: a concept review. *J Addict Dis*, *23*, 39-53.

[116] Bailer, U. F., Narendran, R., Frankle, W. G., Himes, M. L., Duvvuri, V., Mathis, C. A., Kaye, W. H. (2011). Amphetamine induced dopamine release increases anxiety in individuals recovered from anorexia nervosa. *Int J Eat Disord*, In Press.

[117] Lee, A. L., Ogle, W. O., Sapolsky, R. M. (2002). Stress and depression: possible links to neuron death in the hippocampus. *Bipolar Disord*, *4*, 117-28.

[118] Kuo, D. Y. (2003). Further evidence for the mediation of both subtypes of dopamine D1/D2 receptors and cerebral neuropeptide Y (NPY) in amphetamine-induced appetite suppression. *Behav Brain Res*, *147*, 149-55.

In: Anorexia Nervosa ISBN: 978-1-62081-291-4
Editor: N. C. Barbarich-Marsteller

Chapter 7

AVERSION TO FOOD AS AN INHERENT UNDERLYING FACTOR OF ANOREXIA NERVOSA: ANIMAL MODEL PERSPECTIVE

***Pawel K. Olszewski*[*a,b] *and Allen S. Levine*[a]**
[a]Minnesota Obesity Center, Department of Food Science and Nutrition, University of Minnesota, St. Paul, MN, US
[b]Department of Biological Sciences, University of Waikato, Hamilton, New Zealand

ABSTRACT

A common denominator for all anorexia nervosa individuals is rejection of food despite the fact that the organism is in critical need of replenishing energy. Interestingly, not only do hunger mechanisms prove insufficient to stimulate consumption, but also rewarding properties of tastants do not serve as an adequate incentive to motivate eating. In addition, negative associations with consequences of consummatory activity are common in this disease. Intriguingly, food avoidance in anorexia nervosa mirrors characteristic features of taste aversion in animal models: negative associations with food intake cause self-starvation despite hunger and tastant's palatability. Recent studies have shown that taste aversion in rodents is associated with profound changes

* Corresponding author: Pawel K. Olszewski, PhD, Dept. of Biological Sciences, University of Waikato, Private Bag 3105, Hamilton 3240, New Zealand, olsze005@umn.edu

in central expression of genes related to food intake, including genes mediating feeding for energy and those involved in reward. It is particularly striking that administration of ligands that modify reward affects the magnitude of an aversive response, being able to reinforce or, importantly, to alleviate food avoidance. The current chapter offers a perspective on using our knowledge of taste aversion in animal models to better understand the biology of anorexia nervosa and on possible directions in conceptualizing pharmacologic interventions.

INTRODUCTION

One of the most fundamental prerequisites for survival is the ability to obtain enough energy to sustain functioning at the cellular, organismal and behavioral level. This inherent drive to seek and save calories is ensured by complex central and peripheral mechanisms that, among others, propel and maintain food consumption, shift our preference toward high-sugar and/or high-fat foods of high energy density, and allow us to crave certain foods as well as reach gratification of a sated state. In fact, in the modern obesogenic environment, these mechanisms underlie energy overconsumption (that oftentimes leads to obesity) as they have not really evolved to respond to overabundance of food, but rather to its shortage. Hence, anorexia nervosa (AN) - characterized by a host of psychological abnormalities and by voluntary self-starvation despite easy access to food - is a puzzling pathological condition, in which the pro-consummatory activity of feeding mechanisms appears dramatically blunted [1]. Indeed, AN sufferers report somewhat lower hunger ratings and increased self-perceived fullness compared to healthy controls or to individuals with other eating disorders, such as bulimia nervosa. It should be noted, however, that neuroendocrine mediators of hunger, such as CSF neuropeptide Y (NPY) and plasma leptin, tend to be at levels close to a normal range [2]. This may reflect the fact that dysregulation of hunger conveying mechanisms in anorexia is subtle, which allows affected individuals to think - to the extent labeled as even "obsessive" - about food and eating, yet their hunger never translates into the actual consummatory activity [3, 4]. Interestingly, AN individuals reject also palatable tastants and, depending on the progression and type of the disease, they may refuse to consume even those ingestants that are low in or devoid of calories. Therefore, from the standpoint of food intake regulation, the most prominent components of the disease include feeding-related anhedonia [5], nearly complete avoidance of tastants and rapid termination of consumption [3, 4].

Due to the complexity of psychological and physiological manifestations of AN, generation of an animal model accurately reflecting complete symptomology of this eating disorder is virtually impossible. Nonetheless, many research laboratories have attempted to create rodent paradigms in which weight loss would be achieved through a subset of symptoms typical for AN. Activity-based anorexia (ABA) is one of the most commonly used approaches in basic research [6-8]. Rodents are given free access to running wheels while having time-restricted access to food. In response, animals increase wheel running activity and decrease food intake. Consequently, they experience self-imposed starvation and hyperactivity and they fail to meet energy needs. Their weight loss is so dramatic that prolonged continuation of this paradigm may lead to death. The ABA model is very compelling as it encompasses several main features of AN, such as voluntary reduction in energy intake, loss of motivation to eat (it is replaced by a heightened drive to exercise) and emaciation. It does not, however, address one key component of AN: fear associated with a consummatory activity. In AN individuals, this fear stems from dysmorphia and it is related to a self-assessed "risk" of gaining weight [9, 10]. Soon, this fear becomes generalized over activities that may potentially lead to an increased body weight, especially eating behavior, and over food itself. As a result, affected people form an associative link between food intake and negative physical and psychological outcomes, and they learn to avoid food or - if they initiate consumption - to terminate eating activity. This process resembles the formation of aversive responsiveness and, in laboratory animals, it is most closely represented by a learned or conditioned taste aversion (CTA) model [11] which has recently gained attention as a means to decipher physiological and molecular mechanisms underlying certain aspects of anorexia.

In the laboratory setting, a CTA develops when exposure to a specific tastant is followed by an unpleasant consequence (usually a gastrointestinal sensation induced by a concomitant injection of a chemical agent). Upon subsequent presentations, rodents dramatically decrease the intake of this food. When an aversive response is of a great magnitude, this decrease in consumption persists for a long time despite the fact that the tastant may be palatable or that it may be the only source of calories available. In fact, we found that when aversion was induced toward high-fat high-sugar chow which then remained as the only source of energy, rats ate so little of it that we had to replace this chow with food of completely new characteristics, not associated with previous negative experiences [12]. Therefore, just as in AN in humans, in the CTA animal model, food starts being recognized as a potentially dangerous factor and it stays as such for a very long period of time, even though the very negative consequence of consumption (learned via an association) might have occurred only once and it might have been followed by a number of non-negative experiences [13]. Importantly, in CTA animals, rewarding aspects of food intake seem completely absent: aversion powerfully counteracts any reward-related processing of tastants even though they may be palatable and/or may contain calories (hence, may be gratifying by satisfying hunger). Noteworthy, the nature of the relationship between aversion and neuronal activity in central reward circuits which can underlie this sudden displacement within the reward-aversion continuum, has been defined by several authors. For example, Singh and colleagues showed that the nucleus accumbens (NAcc) core and shell are fundamental for proper aversive responding [14]. Roitman et al. found that, in CTA animals exposed to a palatable and avoided tastant, NAcc neurons exhibit a significantly increased firing rate compared to the effect seen in non-CTA controls [15]. The same group of investigators used electrophysiological recordings of NAcc neuronal activity in animals given rewarding (sucrose) versus aversive (quinine) stimuli and concluded that the output of the NAcc is very different in response to those two types of stimulations [16]. Importantly, reward and aversion appear to have their own "dedicated" neurons within the NAcc [16], and this feature likely facilitates an effective and rapid switch from feeding-derived pleasure to food avoidance.

In the aforementioned taste aversion study in rats [12], we utilized real-time PCR to examine expression of genes related to food intake regulation in three major brain areas involved in the control of consummatory responses: the hypothalamus, brain stem and amygdala. We found that, among a number of genes, the ones whose expression levels were altered in the aversive state (corrected for the effect of starvation precipitated by the CTA and the effect of lithium chloride, a drug used to induce aversion) affected either feeding for pleasure alone or both feeding for pleasure and feeding for calories. These genes encode the components of the opioid system, known to promote intake of palatable and caloric fat and sugar as well as non-caloric saccharin [17, 18]; nociceptin/orphanin FQ, closely related to "classical" opioids, which mitigates energy- and reward-related aspects of consumption as well as memory [19, 20]; and melanin concentrating hormone that induces hunger, but also stimulates sugar intake and affects memory/associative processes [21, 22]. It seems, therefore, that food avoidance and readiness for self-inflicted starvation are deeply rooted in the malfunctioning of the molecular systems that affect mainly reward processing, and - to some extent - hunger-driven initiation of consummatory behavior.

What is particularly important for the management of aversive responsiveness is pharmacological interventions employing drugs that target some of the aforementioned systems affecting acquisition of the CTA, its strength and/or time needed for extinction of negative associations with a given diet to diminish. For example, Olszewski et al. showed that agonists of mu, kappa and nociceptin/orphanin FQ (NOP) receptors prevent the development of a lithium chloride-dependent CTA in rats [23]. These ligands also reduced aversion-related activity of hypothalamic and brainstem neurons mediating termination of consummatory behavior, including oxytocin and vasopressin cells. Conversely, an opioid receptor antagonist, naloxone, potentiated the effect of lithium chloride on oxytocin secretion and concomitant anorexia [24]. The blockade of the NOP receptor led to a significantly delayed extinction of a lithium chloride-precipitated CTA and it induced c-Fos immunoreactivity in the central nucleus of the amygdala beyond the level seen when lithium chloride was administered alone in CTA control animals [12]. Finally, an orexigenic antagonist of melanocortin receptors, Agouti-related protein, which has been shown to increase appetitive responding for palatable fat [25], was also found to alleviate aversive symptoms in rats by inhibiting the activity of circuits promoting hypophagia [26].

Despite the existence of persuasive evidence that aversion precipitates anorexigenic responses both short- and long-term and induces a subset of symptoms resembling AN, it is still unclear - because of limitations in creating an ideal animal model of this disease - to what extent and how aversion contributes to anorexia nervosa. Liang et al. have recently published an extremely important study which merges the concept of CTA and ABA [27]. These investigators first induced anorexia by subjecting female rats to the typical ABA protocol with the constant presence of the running wheel and intermittent presentation of food. The animals were then allowed to recover from malnourishment and decreased body weight caused by vigorous exercise and reduced food intake. Subsequently, a CTA paradigm was used in which the rats were given sucrose followed by an injection of very low doses of lithium chloride. The ABA rats acquired a CTA to sugar significantly sooner than the naive controls. Importantly, they completely avoided sucrose while the naive animals still sampled it after ten conditioning sessions. The assessment of CTA extinction revealed that the ABA rats extinguished their aversive responses more slowly than control animals. The data reported by Liang and colleagues clearly demonstrate that AN-like symptoms evoked in both the CTA and ABA models are relevant to our understanding of the disease. Importantly, they show that the occurrence of both sets of symptoms - even if not simultaneously - characterizes an animal chronically vulnerable to sub-threshold levels of stimuli being able to promote self-starvation. It also means that aversive stimuli capable of setting off AN-like manifestations in animals can be very subtle, which is very much in line with findings in humans, where risk factors thought to contribute to negative associations (peer pressure, media influence, dissatisfaction due to skewed self-perception) are oftentimes subtle as well.

CONCLUSION

Follow-up studies are needed to address additional questions stemming from the individual and combined CTA/ABA models, but one of the most crucial conclusions that has emerged from the animal research to date is that food aversion and the associated changes in the activity of the aversion/reward circuits do underlie self-starvation, and their influence is profoundly enhanced if other symptoms of AN have occurred. This emphasizes the importance of conceptualizing experimental pharmacologic treatments for AN that would augment the feeding-related activity of the reward system as well as eradicate accidental negative associations with various diets or flavors.

REFERENCES

[1] Rask-Andersen, M., Olszewski P. K., Levine A. S. & Schioth H. B. (2010) Molecular mechanisms underlying anorexia nervosa: focus on human gene association studies and systems controlling food intake. *Brain Res Rev, 62(2)*, 147-164.

[2] Misra, M. & Klibanski A. (2010) Neuroendocrine consequences of anorexia nervosa in adolescents. *Endocr Dev, 17*, 197-214.

[3] Klein, D. A. & Walsh B. T. (2004) Eating disorders: clinical features and pathophysiology. *Physiol Behav, 81(2)*, 359-374.

[4] Schmidt, U. & Treasure J. (2006) Anorexia nervosa: valued and visible. A cognitive-interpersonal maintenance model and its implications for research and practice. *Br J Clin Psychol, 45(Pt 3)*, 343-366.

[5] Jiang, T., Soussignan R., Rigaud D. & Schaal B. (2010) Pleasure for visual and olfactory stimuli evoking energy-dense foods is decreased in anorexia nervosa. *Psychiatry Res, 180(1)*, 42-47.

[6] Dixon, D. P., Ackert A. M. & Eckel L. A. (2003) Development of, and recovery from, activity-based anorexia in female rats. *Physiol Behav, 80(2-3)*, 273-279.

[7] Beneke, W. M., Schulte S. E. & vander Tuig J. G. (1995) An analysis of excessive running in the development of activity anorexia. *Physiol Behav, 58(3)*, 451-457.

[8] Boakes, R. A., Mills K. J. & Single J. P. (1999) Sex differences in the relationship between activity and weight loss in the rat. *Behav Neurosci, 113(5)*, 1080-1089.

[9] Steinglass, J., Albano A. M., Simpson H. B., Carpenter K., Schebendach J. & Attia E. (2011) Fear of food as a treatment target: Exposure and response prevention for anorexia nervosa in an open series. *Int J Eat Disord.*

[10] Soussignan, R., Jiang T., Rigaud D., Royet J. P. & Schaal B. (2010) Subliminal fear priming potentiates negative facial reactions to food pictures in women with anorexia nervosa. *Psychol Med, 40(3)*, 503-514.

[11] Balagura, S., Brophy J. & Devenport L. D. (1972) Modification of learned aversion to LiCl and NaCl by multiple experiences with LiCl. *J Comp Physiol Psychol, 81(2)*, 212-219.

[12] Olszewski, P. K., Grace M. K., Fard S. S., Le Greves M., Klockars A., Massi M., Schioth H. B. & Levine A. S. (2010) Central nociceptin/orphanin FQ system elevates food consumption by both increasing energy intake and reducing aversive responsiveness. *American journal of physiology Regulatory, integrative and comparative physiology, 299(2)*, R655-663.

[13] Welzl, H., D'Adamo P. & Lipp H. P. (2001) Conditioned taste aversion as a learning and memory paradigm. *Behav Brain Res, 125(1-2)*, 205-213.

[14] Singh, T., McDannald M. A., Haney R. Z., Cerri D. H. & Schoenbaum G. (2010) Nucleus Accumbens Core and Shell are Necessary for Reinforcer Devaluation Effects on Pavlovian Conditioned Responding. *Front Integr Neurosci, 4*, 126.

[15] Roitman, M. F., Wheeler R. A., Tiesinga P. H., Roitman J. D. & Carelli R. M. (2010) Hedonic and nucleus accumbens neural responses to a natural reward are regulated by aversive conditioning. *Learn Mem, 17(11)*, 539-546.

[16] Roitman, M. F., Wheeler R. A. & Carelli R. M. (2005) Nucleus accumbens neurons are innately tuned for rewarding and aversive taste stimuli, encode their predictors, and are linked to motor output. *Neuron, 45(4)*, 587-597.

[17] Barbano, M. F. & Cador M. (2007) Opioids for hedonic experience and dopamine to get ready for it. *Psychopharmacology (Berl), 191(3)*, 497-506.

[18] Gosnell, B. A. & Levine A. S. (2009) Reward systems and food intake: role of opioids. *International journal of obesity, 33 Suppl 2*, S54-58.

[19] Przydzial, M. J. & Heisler L. K. (2008) Nociceptin/orphanin FQ peptide receptor as a therapeutic target for obesity. *Mini Rev Med Chem, 8(8)*, 796-811.

[20] Olszewski, P. K. & Levine A. S. (2004) Minireview: Characterization of influence of central nociceptin/orphanin FQ on consummatory behavior. *Endocrinology, 145(6)*, 2627-2632.

[21] Della-Zuana, O., Presse F., Ortola C., Duhault J., Nahon J. L. & Levens N. (2002) Acute and chronic administration of melanin-concentrating hormone enhances food intake and body weight in Wistar and Sprague-Dawley rats. *Int J Obes Relat Metab Disord, 26(10)*, 1289-1295.

[22] Baird, J. P., Rios C., Gray N. E., Walsh C. E., Fischer S. G. & Pecora A. L. (2006) Effects of melanin-concentrating hormone on licking microstructure and brief-access taste responses. *American journal of physiology Regulatory, integrative and comparative physiology, 291(5)*, R1265-1274.

[23] Olszewski, P. K., Shi Q., Billington C. J. & Levine A. S. (2000) Opioids affect acquisition of LiCl-induced conditioned taste aversion: involvement of OT and VP systems. *American journal of physiology Regulatory, integrative and comparative physiology, 279(4)*, R1504-1511.

[24] Flanagan, L. M., Verbalis J. G. & Stricker E. M. (1988) Naloxone potentiation of effects of cholecystokinin and lithium chloride on oxytocin secretion, gastric motility and feeding. *Neuroendocrinology, 48(6)*, 668-673.

[25] Tracy, A. L., Clegg D. J., Johnson J. D., Davidson T. L. & Benoit S. C. (2008) The melanocortin antagonist AgRP (83-132) increases appetitive responding for a fat, but not a carbohydrate, reinforcer. *Pharmacology, biochemistry, and behavior, 89(3)*, 263-271.

[26] Wirth, M. M., Olszewski P. K., Levine A. S. & Giraudo S. Q. (2002) Effect of Agouti-related protein on development of conditioned taste

aversion and oxytocin neuronal activation. *Neuroreport, 13(10)*, 1355-1358.

[27] Liang, N. C., Bello N. T. & Moran T. H. (2011) Experience with activity based anorexia enhances conditioned taste aversion learning in rats. *Physiology & behavior, 102(1)*, 51-57.

In: Anorexia Nervosa
Editor: N. C. Barbarich-Marsteller ISBN: 978-1-62081-291-4

Chapter 8

A TRANSLATIONAL APPROACH TO UNDERSTANDING ANOREXIA NERVOSA

***Nicole C. Barbarich-Marsteller*[*a,b] *and B. Timothy Walsh*[a,b]**

[a]Department of Psychiatry, College of Physicians and Surgeons of Columbia University, New York, NY, US

[b]New York State Psychiatric Institute, New York, NY, US

ABSTRACT

Anorexia nervosa, with a mortality rate of 5% per decade of illness, ranks among the most lethal of psychiatric disorders.The potential for the development of more effective treatments for this illness would be greatly enhanced if the mechanisms maintaining the abnormal behaviors characteristic of anorexia nervosa were better understood.Preclinical models of human illnesses can provide a unique opportunity to probe physiological mechanisms and to test pharmacotherapies.While it is not possible to fully model the complexity of any psychiatric disorder, an animal model of anorexia nervosa could significantly advance our understanding and treatment of this challenging disorder.This chapter discusses the utility of using a translational model of anorexia nervosa to

* Please send correspondence to: Nicole C. Barbarich-Marsteller, Ph.D., Columbia University, NYSPI, 1051 Riverside Drive, Unit 98, New York, NY 10032, Phone: (212) 543-5197, Fax: (212) 543-5607, nbarbarich@yahoo.com

understand the biology of self-starvation and starvation-induced hyperactivity.

Keywords: anorexia nervosa, activity-based anorexia, eating disorders, animal models, hyperactivity, food restriction

INTRODUCTION

As discussed in the previous chapters of this book, anorexia nervosa is a deadly psychiatric disorder characterized by severe dietary restriction, an unrelenting pursuit of weight loss, symptom fluctuation, and, in many cases, excessive exercise and/or hyperactivity (Chapters 1-3).While there is no clear treatment of choice for individuals with anorexia nervosa during adulthood, family-based treatment appears to be the most efficacious intervention for individuals with anorexia nervosa during adolescence (Chapter 4). Pharmacological treatments have had surprisingly little efficacy during the acute phase of illness or in preventing relapse (Chapter 5).Substantial alterations in brain function exist during starvation and following long-term recovery (Chapter 6),however, the extent to which these alterations are causal remains unclear, as factors that initiate the onset of dieting may be distinct from factors that maintain self-starvation once weight loss has progressed [1].

The largely age- and sex-specific onset of anorexia nervosa in adolescent girls [2] suggests biological and developmental risk factors are involved in the vulnerability for this disorder.Although biological alterations during the course of anorexia nervosa may be found, it is possible that these disturbances may represent acute or chronic effects of starvation, rather than pre-existing factors related to risk.The inability to identify individuals at high risk prior to the onset of illness greatly limits efforts to prevent anorexia nervosa and also makes it difficult to identify pre-existing biological and behavioral factors that increase the vulnerability to developing the illness.The use of a translational model to identify mechanisms that promote self-starvation and hyperactivity holds promise for understanding the unrelenting cycle of weight loss and hyperactivity seen in some individuals with anorexia nervosa.

Activity-based anorexia is an animal model of anorexia nervosa that combines unlimited access to a running wheel with limited access to food, typically for 1 hour per day (Chapter 7; and for example, [3-6]).While the duration of food access is limited, animals can consume as much as they want within the 1 hour period.In many cases, animals do not consume significant amounts of food during the period of food access and instead continue running.This programmed food restriction promotes hyperactivity that results in dramatic weight loss and increasingly greater levels of hyperactivity.Without experimental intervention, many animals with activity-based anorexia will run themselves to death within days, despite the opportunity to consume more food and to minimize activity levels.

Anorexia Nervosa		Activity-Based Anorexia
1. Severe dietary restriction	↔	1. Severe dietary restriction
2. Marked weight loss	↔	2. Marked weight loss
3. Hyperactivity / excessive exercise	↔	3. Hyperactivity / increased wheel running
4. Amenorrhea	↔	4. Loss of estrous cycle
5. Increased vulnerability in adolescent girls	↔	5. Increased vulnerability in adolescent rats
6. Hypothermia due to weight loss	↔	6. Hypothermia due to weight loss
7. Refusal to maintain body weight 8. Intense fear of gaining weight or becoming fat 9. Disturbances in body image	}	Cannot be modeled in the rat

Figure 1. Features of anorexia nervosa and activity-based anorexia.

Figure 1 provides a comparison of the core features associated with anorexia nervosa and activity-based anorexia.The most common species utilized to study activity-based anorexia is the rat, although some more recent studies have utilized mice.The model has been induced across different ages and in both males and females, although evidence suggests that adolescent rats are more vulnerable to activity-based anorexia than adult rats([7]; Barbarich-Marsteller, unpublished data).Our laboratory utilizes adolescent female rats in order to more closely mimic the age- and sex-specific onset of anorexia nervosa in the clinical population[2].Within 3-4 days, most adolescent female rats in our laboratory exhibit severe signs of activity-based anorexia, including significant weight loss (15%-35% of baseline body weight) and hyperactivity (between 6 and 20 km per day or more of wheel running activity, compared to 2 to 4 km per day of wheel running activity in ad lib fed control rats).The majority of animals develop severe behavior that necessitates removal from experimental conditions within several days, although some display resistance to the model, which may itself be useful in identifying protective factors against these maladaptive behaviors.Although it is clear that no animal model can adequately represent all features of a clinical psychiatric disorder, the activity-based anorexia model provides a rational approach for systematically studying the biological mechanisms of weight loss and hyperactivity.

Research identifying the underlying neurobiology driving hyperactivity in the activity-based anorexia model is ongoing (for review, see [8]), as is the examination of factors related to the risk of developing activity-based anorexia and the consequences of activity-based anorexia on subsequent development.While the phenomenon of activity-based anorexia is remarkable and holds significant promise for identifying the biological pathways involved in self-starvation and starvation-induced hyperactivity, it is important to remain critical in translating preclinical findings to a clinical disorder.While characteristics such as dietary restriction, weight loss, hyperactivity, and loss of menstrual cycle function can be modeled in an animal, the psychological disturbances related to body weight and shape and the fear of gaining weight cannot.Moreover, it is also important to recognize that despite behavioral similarities in weight loss and food restriction, the interpretation of similar behaviors across species is challenging, as it is not clear that similar behaviors serve the same neurobiological purpose or are due to the same mechanism.For example, as self-starvation progresses in some individuals with anorexia nervosa, increased exercise may be maintained as a mechanism not only for losing weight, but also for modulating a dysphoric mood.In contrast, while it is unlikely that animals with activity-based anorexia increase wheel running as a mechanism to lose weight, it is unclear whether the continuous wheel running activity may be operating on positive or negative reinforcement, an attempt to maintain body temperature during hypothermia, or another mechanism altogether.Nonetheless, the activity-based anorexia model provides an approach for studying biological factors involved in the development and maintenance of starvation-induced hyperactivity which appears quite similar to the excessive exercise exhibited by many individuals with anorexia nervosa.

The severity of anorexia nervosa and the lack of universally effective treatments provide substantial justification for using a translational approach to identify biological pathways involved in self-starvation and starvation-induced hyperactivity.Future research in our laboratory is aimed at identifying pre-existing biomarkers of vulnerability to developing activity-based anorexia, with the ultimate goal of developing targeted treatments to address the biological disturbances involved in these maladaptive behaviors.Overall, a translational approach to understanding anorexia nervosa holds significant promise for the future.

References

[1] Walsh, B. T., Devlin, M. J. (1998). Eating disorders: progress and problems. *Science,280*, 1387-90.

[2] *American Psychiatric Association. Diagnostic and statistical manual of mental disorders (4th ed., text revision).* Washington, D.C.: American Psychiatric Association; 2000.

[3] Hall J. F., Hanford, P. V. (1954). Activity as a function of a restricted feeding schedule. *J Comp Physiol Psychol,47*, 362-3.

[4] Routtenberg, A., Kuznesof, A. W. (1967). Self-starvation of rats living in activity wheels on a restricted feeding schedule. *J Comp Physiol Psychol,64*, 414-21.

[5] Dixon, D. P., Ackert, A. M., Eckel, L. A. (2003). Development of, and recovery from, activity-based anorexia in female rats. *Physiol Behav,80*, 273-9.

[6] Aoki, C., Sabaliauskas, N., Chowdhury, T., Min, J.Y., Colacino, A.R., Laurino, K., Barbarich-Marsteller, N.C. (2011). Adolescent female rats exhibiting activity-based anorexia express elevated levels of GABA(A) receptor α4 and δ subunits at the plasma membrane of hippocampal CA1 spines. *Synapse,* Epub ahead of print.

[7] Boakes, R. A., Mills, K. J., Single, J. P. (1999). Sex differences in the relationship between activity and weight loss in the rat. *Behav Neurosci,113*, 1080-9.

[8] Adan, R. A., Hillebrand, J. J., Danner, U. N., Cano, S. C., Kas, M. J, Verhagen, L. A. (2011). Neurobiology driving hyperactivity in activity-based anorexia. *Curr Top Behav Neurosci,6*, 229-50.

INDEX

A

D

E

F

G

H

I

L

Q

R

S